The River Gr~~eat~~ ~~Ou~~se and tribut~~aries~~

A guide for river use~~rs~~

The River Great Ouse and The Old West River –
Denver to Bedford
River Wissey, River Little Ouse or Brandon Creek and
River Lark
River Cam and the Cambridgeshire Lodes

ANDREW HUNTER BLAIR
with the assistance of the
Great Ouse Boating Association Ltd

> I've known rivers.
> I've known rivers ancient as the world and
> older than the flow of human blood in human veins.
> My soul has grown deep like the rivers.
> I bathed in the Euphrates when dawn was young.
> I built my hut near the Congo and it lulled me to sleep.
> I raised the pyramids above the Nile
> and I heard the singing of the Mississippi when Abe Lincoln went down to New Orleans,
> and I've seen this beloved bosom turn all golden in the sunset.
> I've known rivers, ancient, dusty rivers.
> My soul has gone deep like the rivers.
>
> B. Hughes
> *Poet Laureate of Harlem*
> (BBC)

Imray Laurie Norie & Wilson Ltd
St Ives Huntingdon England

Published by
Imray, Laurie, Norie & Wilson Ltd
Wych House, St Ives,
Cambridgeshire PE27 5BT, England
☎ (01480) 462114 *Fax* (01480) 496109
E-mail ilnw@imray.com
2004

© Andrew Hunter Blair 2004
© Imray Laurie Norie & Wilson Ltd 2004

Mapping.
Reproduced by permission of Ordnance
Survey on behalf of The Controller of Her
Majesty's Stationery Office © Crown
Copyright

British Library Cataloguing in Publication
Data.
A catalogue record for this book is available
from the British Library.

ISBN 0 85288 800 7

CAUTION
Every effort has been taken to ensure the
accuracy of this book. It contains selected
information and thus is not definitive and
does not include all known information on
the subject in hand; this is particularly
relevant to the plans which should not be
used for navigation. The author and
publisher believe that its selection is a useful
aid to prudent navigation but the safety of a
vessel depends ultimately on the judgement
of the navigator who should assess all
information, published or unpublished,
available to him.

This work has been corrected to April 2004

Printed in Great Britain by
Imray Laurie Norie & Wilson Ltd

KEY TO SYMBOLS USED ON THE MAPS

Scale approximately
5 cm to 1 kilometre
3″ to 1 mile

Bridge heights are taken at normal river levels

	Slipway
	Direction of stream
⊠	Post Office
☎	Telephone
≫	Lock
=	Weir
i	Information
	Pump-out
WC	Toilet
	Public House
	Fuel
	Water
	Church
	Station
	Showers
·••••	Power Cable
- - - -	Footpath
GS	General Store
E.Cl.	Early Closing
F&C	Fish and Chips
U/S	Upstream
D/S	Downstream
M	Miles
km	Kilometres
But	Butcher

Contents

Pole Star 57'
17.5 m.

Contents

River Great Ouse
The Wash to Denver

Distance	25.7km (16 miles)
Length	Unrestricted
Beam	Unrestricted
Draught	1.8m (6') (tidal)
Headroom	2.3m (7' 8") (min)
Locks	1 (Denver)

The River Great Ouse and
Old West River
Denver to Earith

Distance	50km (31.1 miles)
Length	30m (98' 5")
Beam	4m (13' 1")
Draught	1m (3' 3") (min)
Headroom	2.9m (9' 6")
Locks	1

River Great Ouse
Earith to Kempston Mill, Bedford

Distance	65.2km (40.5 miles)
Length	25.0m (82')
Beam	3.3m (10' 10")
Draught	1m (3' 3")
Headroom	2.2m (7' 3") (2.4m (8' 1") to Priory Marina, Bedford)
Locks	15

New Bedford River
Denver to Earith

Distance	33.5km (20.8 miles)
Length	Unrestricted
Beam	Unrestricted
Draught	0.6m (2') (tidal)
Headroom	2.3m (7' 10") (min)
Locks	None

Old Bedford River
Welche's Dam to Old Bedford
Sluice

Distance	19.8km (12.3 miles)
Length	Unrestricted
Beam	4.5m (15')
Draught	1m (3' 6")
Headroom	2.4m (8') HWS
Locks	1

River Wissey
Great Ouse to Whittington

Distance	18km (11.2 miles)
Length	15m (49' 3")
Beam	4m (13'1")
Draught	1m (3' 3")
Headroom	2.4 m (7' 9")
Locks	None

River Little Ouse or Brandon
Creek
Great Ouse to Brandon

Distance	22km (13.7 miles)
Length	12m (39' 4")
Beam	3.5m (11' 6")
Draught	1.2m (3' 11")
Headroom	2m (6' 7")
Locks	1

Earith Sluice
Earith ⦁ ✕
(Tidal between locks)
Brownshill   Hermita
Staunch   ⌐Lock
Houghton
Lock Hemingford
HUNTINGDON   Lock
⦁   ⦁ **Godman-**   ⦁**St. Ives**
Brampton   **chester**   St Ives Lock
Lock ↘
Godmanchester **Hemingfords**
Lock

Offord Lock ↘

St. Neots Lock ↘

ST. NEOTS
↙ Eaton Socon Lock

Barford

River Great Ouse

↙ Roxton Lock

Castle Mills
Lock   ↙ Great Barford Lock
BEDFORD
↘ Willington Lock
Bedford Cardington Lock
Lock

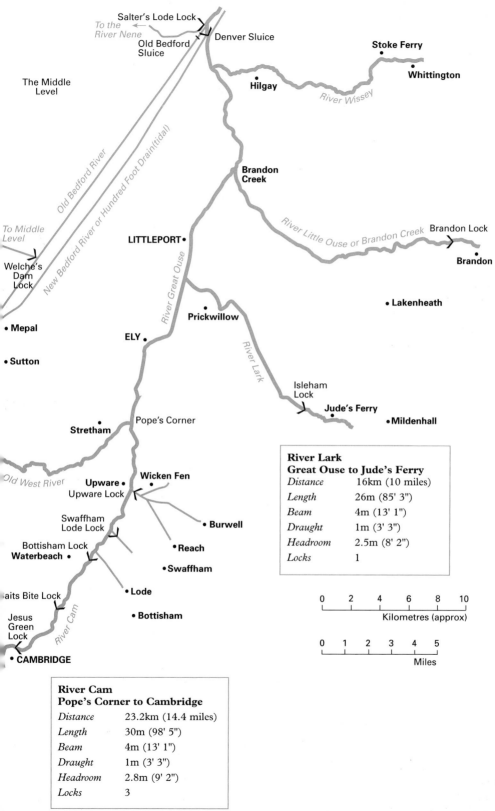

Salter's Lode Lock

To the
River Nene ←

Denver Sluice

Old Bedford
Sluice

Stoke Ferry

Whittington

The Middle
Level

Hilgay

River Wissey

Old Bedford River

New Bedford River or Hundred Foot Drain(tidal)

Brandon
Creek

River Little Ouse or Brandon Creek

Brandon Lock

Brandon

To Middle
Level

LITTLEPORT•

Welche's
Dam
Lock

River Great Ouse

• **Mepal**

ELY •

Prickwillow

• **Lakenheath**

River Lark

• **Sutton**

Isleham
Lock

Jude's Ferry •

•**Mildenhall**

Stretham

Pope's Corner

Old West River

Wicken Fen

Upware •
Upware Lock

• **Burwell**

Swaffham
Lode Lock

Bottisham Lock
Waterbeach •

•**Reach**

•**Swaffham**

aits Bite Lock

River Cam

• **Lode**

Jesus
Green
Lock

• **Bottisham**

• **CAMBRIDGE**

River Lark
Great Ouse to Jude's Ferry

Distance	16km (10 miles)
Length	26m (85' 3")
Beam	4m (13' 1")
Draught	1m (3' 3")
Headroom	2.5m (8' 2")
Locks	1

```
0     2     4     6     8    10
├──┴──┴──┴──┴──┴──┴──┴──┴──┴──┤
          Kilometres (approx)
```

```
0    1    2    3    4    5
├──┴──┴──┴──┴──┴──┴──┴──┴──┤
                      Miles
```

River Cam
Pope's Corner to Cambridge

Distance	23.2km (14.4 miles)
Length	30m (98' 5")
Beam	4m (13' 1")
Draught	1m (3' 3")
Headroom	2.8m (9' 2")
Locks	3

Navigation

The Environment Agency (EA) is generally responsible for the management of navigation on the River Great Ouse and its tributaries. There is one exception namely that part of the River Cam upstream from Bottisham Lock where this responsibility passes to the Cam Conservancy. Their laws, byelaws and regulations are designed to ensure, as far as is reasonably practical, the safety and mutual enjoyment of the river by all.

River cruising is relaxing and enjoyable. The way of life should be unhurried, courteous and respectful of all other river users. A slow, sensible and considerate approach will help to maintain this tradition. Boat wash is perhaps the single most damaging aspect of river cruising. It can damage banks and passing and moored craft, cause injury and upset smaller craft. Watch the wash and slow down. There are some simple rules of the road.

- Keep to the speed limits
- Keep to the right when passing approaching craft
- Overtake on the left
- Never overtake near bends, bridges, approaching craft or moored craft
- Slow down and give way to sailing boats
- Slow down when approaching other craft, bridges and narrows
- Try to avoid anglers' fishing lines
- Be alert and keep a sharp lookout
- Use sound signals as required
  One short blast - I am steering to starboard
  Two short blasts - I am steering to port
  Three short blasts − My engines are going astern

Public moorings, usually free, are provided by the Environment Agency and certain local authorities. Hotels and inns generally offer free moorings to their patrons. Most marinas and some riparian owners provide moorings for a small charge. The Great Ouse Boating Association (GOBA) offers free mooring to its members. Here are some basic mooring guidelines.

- Do not leave it too late
- Moor facing upstream
- Do not allow mooring lines and stakes to form unforeseen hazards
- Always leave moorings clean and tidy

Locks, whilst being hazardous and requiring care, are often very sociable places and form part of the enjoyment of river cruising.

- Approach locks slowly
- If full or closed, moor at the landing stages
- Watch for currents, eddies and wind effects
- Follow any instructions – if in doubt seek help
- Ensure gates and paddles are in the correct positions before operation
- Always open paddles and gates slowly, a little at a time
- Before leaving upstream, close the upstream paddles
- Be alert and keep a sharp lookout

Explosion is the principal risk aboard. Petrol vapour can spread a long way and gas fumes can collect in the bottom of the boat.

- When refuelling, extinguish all naked lights and no smoking
- When changing gas bottles, turn off all appliances and no smoking
- Ensure that there are sufficient modern fire extinguishers
- Know where fire extinguishers and fire blankets are installed
- Know where the cabin exits are situated

For the comfort and safety of all on board, non-slip shoes should be worn and there should be a supply of dry, warm and waterproof clothes. Life-jackets should always be worn by children and non-swimmers.

- Know the location of life-belts
- Plan for and practise 'man overboard'
- Ensure that all on board know how to put the engine into neutral

BOAT LICENSING AND REGISTRATION

All craft using the River Great Ouse and associated waterways are obliged to hold an up to date river licence.

Details of regional requirements for the registration and licensing of craft to use the Rivers Great Ouse and Cam and associated EA controlled waterways are available from:

The Environment Agency
Anglian Region
Kingfisher House
Goldhay Way
Orton Goldhay
Peterborough PE2 5ZR
☎ 01733 371811

Boat owners navigating recreational waterways within EA Anglian Region should acquaint themselves with the following legislation, copies of which can be obtained from the EA at the above address.

The Recreational Waterways (Registration) Byelaws 1979
The Recreational Waterways (General) Byelaws 1980
The Recreational Waterways (Parks) Byelaws 1981

EA ANGLIAN REGION DISTRICT OFFICES

Telephone numbers refer to office hours
Central Area
Bromholme Lane, Brampton, Huntingdon
☎ 01480 414581
Tidal Ouse
Denver to Stowbridge
EA King's Lynn
☎ 01553 760607

Note

Outside office hours contact ☎ 0800 80 70 60. In either case emergencies will be dealt with immediately. If a resolution of the problem is likely to be delayed, the caller will be contacted and appraised of the situation.

Introduction

The River Great Ouse rises near Brackley in Northamptonshire and flows through Bedford, St Neots, Huntingdon, St Ives, Earith, Ely, Littleport and Denver on its 260km course to the Wash at King's Lynn. On its way it is joined by the River Cam which rises south of Cambridge, the Roman Cambridgeshire Lodes, and the Rivers Lark, Little Ouse, Wissey and Nar. Whilst the upper reaches are natural watercourses meandering in wide flood plains, the lower reaches, often man-made, flow within artificial flood banks across the lower-lying fenland. They all carry water originating from higher lands in the south and east and enable the fens, over which they cross in the lower reaches, to be drained. For the most part the rivers are fluvial; however the Great Ouse is tidal from Brownshill Staunch to Earith, from Earith along the New Bedford River and from Denver to King's Lynn.

The rivers are navigable up to Bedford, Cambridge, Jude's Ferry near Isleham, Brandon and Stoke Ferry. The two tidal sections require special expertise in the lower reaches. Stretches of the rivers Lark, Little Ouse and Wissey are prone to heavy weed growth during the summer. By crossing the Middle Level from near Denver to Peterborough and travelling up the River Nene to Northampton, it is possible to join the Grand Union Canal and its network of canals.

The rivers, rich in history and folklore, are peaceful and picturesque. This guide gives a brief history of the development of the river system and an account of the principal attractions within the corridor of the rivers. It will be of interest to all river users, particularly navigators and walkers on the Ouse Valley Way, the Fen River Way and the many footpaths along the river banks.

REFERENCES AND FURTHER READING

The Author gratefully acknowledges the following references, further reading and maps which have been used extensively when researching the back-ground to this guide.

A Geology for Engineers F G H Blyth. Arnold 1961

Geology and Scenery in England and Wales A E Trueman. Pelican 1963

Roman Britain and Early England P Hunter Blair. Sphere Books 1975

Anglo Saxon England P Hunter Blair. Cambridge Univ. Press 1956

The Anglo Saxon Chronicle Trl. G N Garmonsway. Dent 1953

The Medieval Fenland H C Darby. David and Charles 1974

Lord Orford's Voyage Around the Fens Intr. H J K Jenkins. Cambs Library Publs 1987

Vermuyden and the Fens L E Harris. Cleaver Hume 1953

Old Houses and Village Buildings in East Anglia B Oliver. Batsford 1912

The Ancient Bridges of Mid and Eastern England E Jervoise. The Architectural Press 1932

Fenland Rivers I Wedgewood. Rich and Cowan 1936

Rivers of East Anglia J Turner. Cassell 1954

Fenland River R Tibbs. Dalton 1969.

The Great Ouse D Summers. David and Charles 1973

Fenland Waterways M Roulstone. Balfour 1974

The Great Level D Summers. David and Charles 1976

The Middle Level A Map and Commentary A Hunter Blair. Imray Laurie Norie and Wilson 2000

The Fenland Past and Present S H Miller & S B J Skertchley. Longmans 1878

The Draining of the Fens H C Darby. Cambridge Univ. Press 1940

The Fens A Bloom. Robert Hale 1953

Portrait of the Fen Country E Storey. Hale 1972

The Black Fens A K Astbury. E P Publishing 1973

Liable to Floods J R Ravensdale. Cambridge Univ. Press 1974

The Changing Fenland H C Darby. Cambridge Univ. Press 1983

East Anglia D Wallace. Batsford 1939

East Anglia P Steggall. Robert Hale 1979

East Anglia H Innes. Hodder and Stoughton 1986

Victoria History of the Counties of England, Cambridgeshire. 1953

Cambridgeshire A Mee. Hodder and Stoughton 1939

Cambridgeshire E A R Ennion. Robert Hale 1951

The Buildings of England, Cambridgeshire N Pevsner. Penguin Books 1954

The Cambridgeshire Landscape C Taylor. Hodder and Stoughton 1973

A View of Cambridgeshire M Rouse. Dalton 1974

Cambridgeshire, A Shell Guide N Scarfe. Faber and Faber 1983

Norfolk A Mee. Hodder and Stoughton 1940.

The Buildings of North West and South Norfolk N Pevsner. Penguin Books 1962

Norfolk Villages D H Kennett. Robert Hale 1980

Suffolk and Norfolk M R James. Dent 1930

Suffolk, A Shell Guide N Scarfe. Faber and Faber 1976

A History of Huntingdonshire M Wickes. Phillimore 1985.

The Book of Huntingdon C Dunn. Hollen Street Press 1990

Godmanchester H J M Green. Oleander Press 1977

The Buildings of England, Bedfordshire and the County of Huntingdon and Peterborough N Pevsner. Penguin Books 1974

Bedfordshire and Huntingdonshire Landscape P Bigmore. Hodder and Stoughton 1979.

Bedfordshire and Huntingdonshire A Mee. Hodder and Stoughton 1973.

Victoria History of the Counties of England, Bedfordshire. Univ. of London Inst. of Historical Research 1972

The Skaters of the Fens A Bloom. Heffer 1958

Curiosities of Rural Cambridgeshire P Jeever. Oleander Press 1977

Cambridgeshire Customs and Folklore E Porter. Routledge & Kegan Paul 1969

Tales from the Fens W H Barrett. Routledge and Kegan Paul 1963

Forgotten Railways of East Anglia R S Joby. David and Charles 1977

Inland Cruising, Practical Course Notes. Royal Yachting Association 1995

Navigations in the Anglian Region Environment Agency

MAPS

British Geological Survey. England and Wales, Solid and Drift.
Sheet 158 Peterborough (1984)
Sheet 159 Wisbech (1995)
Sheet 172 Ramsey (1995)

Sheet 173 Ely (1980)
Sheet 188 Cambridge (1981)
Ordnance Survey *Explorer* 1:25000 maps
208   Bedford & St Neots
209   Cambridge
225   Huntingdon & St Ives
226   Ely & Newmarket
228   March & Ely
236   King's Lynn, Downham Market &
      Swaffham

USEFUL TELEPHONE NUMBERS
Middle Level Commissioners, March
   ☎ 01354 653232
Environment Agency:
Denver lock-keeper ☎ 01366 382340
Salter's Lode lock-keeper ☎ 01366 382292
Stanground lock-keeper ☎ 01733 566413
Ely ☎ 01353 666660
Peterborough ☎ 01733 371811
Huntingdon ☎ 01480 414581
Fens Tourism Group, Spalding ☎ 01775
   762715
Fenland District Council ☎ 01354 654321

USEFUL ADDRESSES
Environment Agency, Kingfisher House,
   Orton Goldhay, Peterborough PE2 5ZR
   ☎ 01733 371811 (24 hours)
Environment Agency, Bromholm Lane,
   Brampton, Huntingdon PE18 8NE
   ☎ 01480 414581 (local office)
Environmental Incidents 24-hour
   emergency line ☎ 0800 80 70 60
**Great Ouse Boating Association
   (GOBA)**, PO Box 244, Huntingdon
   PE29 6FE
   E-mail membership@ goba.org.uk
River Cam Conservancy, Archer and
   Archer, Market Place, Ely, Cambs ☎
   01353 662203
Middle Level Commissioners, Middle
   Level Offices, Dartford Road, March,
   Cambs ☎ 01354 653232

TOURIST INFORMATION CENTRES
Bedford, St Paul's Square, Bedford
   ☎ 01234 215226
Ely, Oliver Cromwell's House, 29 St
   Mary's Street, Ely, Cambs CB7 4HF
   ☎ 01353 662062
Cambridge, Wheeler Street, Cambridge
   CB2 3QB ☎ 01223 322640
St Ives, The Library, Station Rd, St Ives
   ☎ 01480 398004
Huntingdon, Huntingdon Library, Princes
   Street, Huntingdon ☎ 01480 388588
St Neots, St Neots Museum, 8 New Street,
   St Neots, Huntingdon ☎ 01480 388785

BOAT CLUBS AND MARINAS ON THE GREAT OUSE AND CAM
Barford Boat Yard, New Road, Great
Barford, Bedfordshire ☎ 01234 870401
Bedford Boat Club, Mrs S. West, 59
Tythe Barn Road, Wootton, Beds MK43
9EZ ☎ 01234 768530
Brearley Marina, St Neots, Huntingdon,
Cambridgeshire ☎ 01480 472411
Bridge Boatyard, Ely, Cambridgeshire
☎ 01353 663726
The Buckden Marina, Buckden,
Huntingdon, Cambridgeshire
☎ 01480 810355
Cambridge Motor Boat Club,
Waterbeach, Cambridgeshire
☎ 01223 860149
**Cambridgeshire Marine Industries
Association**, Mrs Syred (Sec), Fox's
Boatyard, 10 Marina Drive, March,
Cambridgeshire PE15 0AY
☎ 01354 652770
Carters Boatyard, Mill Road Buckden,
Huntingdon, Cambridgeshire
☎ 01480 811503
Crosshall Marina, Crosshall Road, St
Neots, Huntingdon, Cambridgeshire
☎ 01480 472763
Daylock Marine, Hartford Road, Wyton,
Huntingdon, Cambridgeshire
☎ 01480 455898
Denver Cruising Club, Old Ferry Boat
Inn, Southery, Norfolk ☎ 01353 676310
Dick Clark, Boatbuilders, Stretham,
Cambridgeshire ☎ 01353 649476
Fish and Duck Marina, Overcote Ferry,
Stretham, Ely, Cambridgeshire
☎ 01353 649580
C Fox (Boatbuilders), 10 Marina Drive,
March, Cambridgeshire ☎ 01354 652770
Great Ouse Boating Association, PO
Box 244, Huntingdon PE18 6FE
E-mail membership@ goba.org.uk
Hartford Marina, Banks End, Hartford
Road, Wyton, Huntingdon, Cambridgeshire
☎ 01480 454677
Hermitage Marina, Earith, Huntingdon,
Cambridgeshire☎ 01487 840994
Huntingdon Boat Haven,
Godmanchester, Huntingdon,
Cambridgeshire ☎ 01480 411977
Huntingdon Boat Club, ☎ 01480 456963
Huntingdon Marine and Leisure,
Godmanchester, Huntingdon,
Cambridgeshire ☎ 01480 413517
Isleham Marina, Fenbank, Isleham,
Cambridgeshire ☎ 01638 780663

L. H. Jones & Son Ltd, The Boathaven, St Ives, Huntingdon, Cambridgeshire ☎ 01480 494040
Kelpie Marine, Al Roxton, Bedford MK44 3DS ☎ 01234 870249
Littleport Boat Haven, Littleport, Ely, Cambridgeshire ☎ 01353 863763
Loveys Marine, Ely Marina, Waterside, Ely, Cambridgeshire ☎ 01353 664622
Mr Daymond Hire Boats, 4 Spruce Road, Clackclose Park, Downham Market ☎ 01366 383618 or 01366 384404
Norman Cole Marine, Upware, Ely, Cambridgeshire ☎ 01223 860528
Ouse Valley River Club ☎ 01480 683538
Pike & Eel Marina, Overcote Road, Needingworth, Cambridgeshire ☎ 01480 463336
Priory Marina, Barkers Lane, Bedford MK41 9DJ ☎ 01234 351931
Purvis Marine, Hartford Road, Huntingdon, Cambridgeshire ☎ 01480 453628
Quiet Waters Boat Haven, Earith, Huntingdon, Cambridgeshire ☎ 01487 842154
Richard Allen Boat Sales at Westview Marina, Earith, Huntingdon ☎ 01487 740010
River Mill, School Lane, Eaton Socon St Neots, Huntingdon, Cambridgeshire ☎ 01480 473456
St Ives Pilotage Co. ☎ 01480 462555 for pilot in the tidal river and The Wash
St Neots Marina, South Street, St Neots, Huntingdon, Cambridgeshire ☎ 01480 472411
Two Tees Boatyard, 70 Water Street, Cambridge ☎ 01223 365597
Upware Marine (Trebleways) Ltd, Upware, Ely, Cambridgeshire ☎ 01353 721930
Westview Marina, Earith, Huntingdon, Cambridgeshire ☎ 01487 841627

PUBLIC LAUNCHING SITES
River Great Ouse
Denver
Ely (Waterside)
St Ives (on quay D/S of bridge and by church)
Huntingdon (D/S of Purvis Marine by Rowing Club)
Godmanchester (The Causeway)
St Neots by rowing club
Barford (Anchor pub)
River Wissey
Hilgay D/S of road bridge

River Little Ouse
Brandon D/S of Brandon Staunch. Light craft only
Tidal River Great Ouse
King's Lynn Common Staithe Quay
River Cam
Upware; Five Miles from Anywhere P.H.

TOILET PUMP-OUT SERVICES
River Great Ouse
River Mill, School Lane, Eaton Socon, St Neots, Cambridgeshire ☎ 01480 473456
Buckden Marina, Buckden, Huntingdon, Cambridgeshire ☎ 01480 810355
Denver Sluice (EA)
Ely Willow Walk (EA)
Hartford Marina, Hartford Road, Wyton, Huntingdon, Cambridgeshire ☎ 01480 454677
Westview Marina (EA) ☎ 01487 841627
Hermitage Marina, Earith, Huntingdon, Cambridgeshire ☎ 01487 840994
Littleport (EA)
Jesus Green, Cambridge (EA)

GOBA MOORINGS
The descriptions RH and LH refer to the banks as seen from craft cruising downstream
River Great Ouse and Old West
Fish and Duck
RH bank between the railway bridge and the Fish and Duck footbridge.
Lazy Otter (Old West)
LH bank for approx 120m downstream from fence enclosing PH moorings.
Aldreth Drain (Old West)
LH bank 200m upstream from High Bridge.
Pike and Eel, Overcote Ferry
LH bank immediately upstream from entrance to Pike and Eel Marina. 200m in length.
Noble's Field, St Ives
LH bank between St Ives and Hemingford Lock.
Hemingford Meadow
RH bank between Hemingford Grey and Hemingford Abbots.
Brampton
LH bank between railway bridge and Brampton Mill.
Mailer's Meadow
LH bank between Brampton Lock and Buckden Marina.
Offord
RH bank adjacent to landing stage downstream from lock.
Great Barford
RH bank between the lock and bridge.

Goldington
LH bank downstream from old railway bridge.
Priory Marina
Enquire at Reception.
River Wissey
Grange Farm, Wittington
LH bank about 0.4km above Stoke Ferry, imediately through new road bridge.
River Lark
Isleham Marina
LH bank upstream from lock.
River Cam
Dimmock's Cote
RH bank 170m upstream from Dimmock's Cote Bridge.
The Lodes
Wicken Fen
LH bank at junction of Wicken Lode and Monk's Lode.
Reach Lode
Villae.

The use of GOBA moorings is free to members and hirers of craft operated by GOBA.
There is a maximum stay of 48 hours.
Boats take priority over fishing. A reminder that fishing without a licence is an offence prosecuted by the EA and policed by water bailiffs and EA enforcement officers. The maximum fine is £2500.
Moor as close as possible to other boats and close up gaps if necessary. Help fellow members to find space or raft onto your boat at busy times.
Keep children and animals under proper control. There are often farm animals where moorings are on fields.
Do not light ground fires.
Pick up litter and dog mess.
Do not tie your ropes to GOBA mooring signs.
Members are reminded that the use of GOBA moorings are at 'own risk' and you are advised to have third party liability insurance.

ENVIRONMENT AGENCY MOORINGS
The descriptions RH and LH refer to the banks as seen from craft cruising downstream
River Great Ouse and Old West
Denver
LH bank upstream from Jenyn's Arms.
Ten Mile Bank
Both banks upstream from Hilgay Bridge on River Great Ouse.
Brandon Creek
RH bank beside picnic area upstream from the Ship.

Littleport
Both banks between A10 road bridge and Littleport Boathaven.
Littleport
RH bank downstream from Sandhill's road bridge.
Queen Adelaide
RH bank immediately upstream from road and rail bridges.
Ely
Two moorings separated by the entrance to Bridge Boatyard on LH bank between the road and railway bridges, upstream from Ely Riverside.
Little Thetford
LH bank downstream from junction of Rivers Cam and Old West.
Stretham (Old West)
LH bank 100m beyond bridge upstream from Stretham Engine.
Earith
LH bank adjacent to Westview Marina.
The Dolphin, St. Ives
In cut on RH bank immediately upstream from the Dolphin Hotel.
Houghton
On island forming LH bank of main river downstream from Houghton Lock. NB no access by land.
Godmanchester
Old lock walls adjacent to new lock.
Great Barford
LH bank immediately downstream from bridge.
Old Mills
On island forming LH bank of backwater.
River Wissey
Hilgay
RH bank through second bridge in village.
Little Ouse or Brandon Creek
Brandon Downstream from Brandon Lock on LH bank next to playing field.
Brandon Town
RH bank upstream from road bridge.
River Lark
River Lark
LH bank about 0·8km from junction with River Great Ouse.
Prickwillow
LH bank between road and railway bridges in village.
The Lodes *for At the end of perry moorings, abo Upward Lock*
Burwell
RH bank at end of navigation.

Environment Agency Moorings are free to all river users and most carry a 48 hour limit.

DISTANCES

RIVER GREAT OUSE AND OLD WEST RIVER

All distances and dimensions should be treated only as a guide.

	Km	(miles)
The Wash, mouth of river, to		
Denver Sluice	25.8	(16.0)
Denver Sluice to:		
Junction with River Wissey	1.7	(1.1)
Southery Ferry	9.2	(5.7)
Brandon Creek, junction with River Little Ouse	10.9	(6.8)
Littleport Bridge	17.0	(10.6)
Junction with River Lark	19.6	(12.2)
Cutter Inn, Ely	25.9	(16.1)
Pope's Corner, junction with River Cam	31.3	(19.5)
Stretham Ferry	35.8	(22.3)
Twenty Pence Ferry	38.6	(24.0)
Aldreth Bridge	44.5	(27.7)
Hermitage Lock	50.0	(31.1)
Brownshill Staunch	53.8	(33.4)
Holywell	58.3	(36.2)
St Ives Lock	62.1	(38.6)
Hemingford Lock	64.9	(40.3)
Houghton Lock	67.4	(41.9)
Hartford	69.8	(43.3)
Huntingdon	71.8	(44.6)
Godmanchester Lock	72.9	(45.3)
Brampton Lock	75.0	(46.6)
Offord Lock	79.8	(49.6)
Great Paxton	83.2	(51.7)
St Neots Lock	85.9	(53.4)
St Neots	88.0	(54.7)
Eaton Socon Lock	89.3	(55.5)
Little Barford	91.9	(57.1)
Tempsford Bridge	95.6	(59.4)
Roxton Lock	96.7	(60.1)
Great Barford Lock	100.4	(62.4)
Willington Lock	102.8	(63.9)
Castle Mills Lock	106.4	(66.1)
Cardington Lock	109.0	(67.7)
Bedford Town Lock	111.7	(69.4)
Bedford	112.2	(69.7)
Kempston Mill, limit of navigation	116.2	(72.2)

Headroom under Bridges

Denver Sluice Road Bridge	4.6m	(15' 2")
Denver Sluice Foot Bridge	4.7m	(15' 6")
Railway Bridge	4.0m	(13' 2")
Hilgay Toll Bridge	3.4m	(11' 3")
Littleport Bridge	3.4m	(11' 2")
Sandhills Bridge	3.4m	(11' 2")
Adelaide Road Bridge	3.6m	(11' 10")
Adelaide Railway Bridge	3.6m	(11' 10")
New road Bridge	3.6m	(11' 10")
Beet Factory Footbridge	3.5m	(11' 6")
Muckhill Railway Bridge	3.3m	(10' 10")
Ely Marina Bridge	3.2m	(10' 6")
Cutter Railway Bridge	3.3m	(10' 10")
Ely High Bridge	3.3m	(10' 10")
Newmarket Railway Bridge	3.3m	(10' 10")
Fish and Duck Bridge		
Old West	4.0m	(13' 2")
Railway Bridge	3.6m	(11' 8")
A1123 Road Bridge	3.2m	(10' 6")
Stretham Wooden Bridge	3.5m	(11' 6")
Stretham Ferry	3.2m	(10' 6")
A10 Bridge	3.0m	(9' 10")
Twenty Pence	3.3m	(10' 4")
Aldreth	3.2m	(10' 6")
Willingham Flat Bridge	3.6m	(11' 8")
St Ives New Bridge	4.1m	(13' 5")
St Ives Town Bridge	2.7m	(8' 10")
Hemingford Lock Bridge	2.7m	(8' 10")
Huntingdon Town Bridge	3.4m	(11' 2")
Railway Bridge	4.8m	(15' 9")
Offord Lock Bridge	2.5m	(8' 1")
St Neots Paper Mill Bridge	2.9m	(9' 5")
St Neots Town Bridge	2.8m	(9' 2")
Eaton Socon Lock Bridge	2.7m	(9' 0")
Tempsford New Road Bridge	3.7m	(12' 0")
Tempsford Old Road Bridge	3.1m	(10' 1")
Barford Bridge	3.0m	(9' 9")
Sewage Works Bridge	2.6m	(8' 8")
Road and Pipe Bridge	2.7m	(8' 10")
Bedford Marina Entrance	2.7m	(8' 10")
Railway Bridge	2.3m	(7' 6")
Footbridge	2.9m	(9' 6")
Bedford Inner Relief Road Bridge	2.7m	(8' 10")
Footbridge	2.1m	(7' 0")

NEW BEDFORD OR HUNDRED FOOT RIVER (tidal)

	Km	(miles)
Denver Sluice to:		
Welney Suspension Bridge	9.7	(6.0)
Oxlode	18.2	(11.3)
Mepal Bridge	24.8	(15.4)
Sutton Bridge	26.9	(16.7)
River Great Ouse at Earith	32.7	(20.3)

Headroom under bridges at High Water Spring Tide

Welney Bridge	2.4m	(7' 10")
Railway Bridge	2.7m	(8' 10")
Mepal Bridge	3.3m	(10'10")
Sutton Gault	2.9m	(9' 6")
Earith	4.1m	(13' 5")

RIVER WISSEY

Junction with River Great Ouse to:

	Km	(miles)
Hilgay New Road Bridge	3.4	(2.1)
Wissington Light Railway Bridge	7.9	(4.9)
Wissington Sugar Beet Wharf	8.2	(5.1)
Wissington Road Bridge	8.4	(5.2)
Lode to Methwold Common	10.6	(6.6)
Lode to Stoke Ferry Fen	11.1	(6.9)
Methwold Lode	11.6	(7.2)
Lode to Northwold Fen	12.7	(7.9)
Siphon over Cut-Off Channel	13.2	(8.2)
Bridge to Stoke Ferry Fen	13.5	(8.4)
Branch to Cut-Off Channel	13.7	(8.5)
Stoke Ferry Bridge (A134)	14.5	(9.0)
Whittington	16.1	(10.0)
Limit of Navigation	16.9	(10.5)

Headroom under Bridges

Hilgay Railway Bridge	2.7m	(8' 8")
Hilgay Road Bridge	2.6m	(8' 4")
Wissington Light Railway Bridge	3.0m	(9' 10")
Wissington Beet Factory Pipe	3.2m	(10' 6")
Wissington Road Bridge	3.5m	(11' 6")
Wissey Sluice Bridge	2.9m	(9' 6")
Stoke Ferry Road Bridge (A134)	2.9m	(9' 6")

RIVER LITTLE OUSE or BRANDON CREEK

Junction with River Great Ouse to:

	Km	(miles)
Little Ouse Bridge	3.2	(2.0)
Redmere Bridge	6.4	(4.0)
Botany Bay	8.9	(5.5)
Junction with Lakenheath Lode	9.7	(6.0)
Wilton Bridge	15.3	(9.5)
Cut-Off Channel Syphon	15.9	(9.9)
Junction with Cut-Off Channel	16.1	(10.0)
Railway Bridge	20.1	(12.5)
Brandon Staunch	21.6	(13.4)
Brandon Bridge	22.0	(13.7)

Headroom under Bridges

Brandon Creek Bridge	3.1m	(10' 2")
St John's Road Bridge	3.2m	(10' 4")
Redmere Bridge	3.0m	(9' 10")
Wilton Bridge	3.3m	(10' 10")
Sluice Bridge	2.6m	(8' 6")

RIVER LARK

Junction with River Great Ouse to:

	Km	(miles)
Railway Bridge	3.1	(1.9)
Prickwillow Bridge	3.4	(2.1)
Isleham Lock	13.0	(8.1)
Jude's Ferry Bridge, limit of navigation	16.3	(10.1)

Headroom under Bridges

Branch Bridge	3.4m	(11' 2")
Prickwillow Railway Bridge	3.1m	(10' 1")
Prickwillow Road Bridge	3.0m	(9' 9")
Jude's Ferry Road Bridge	3.2m	(10' 6")

RIVER CAM

Pope's Corner to:

	Km	(miles)
Upware, junction with Reach and Burwell Lodes	5.0	(3.1)
Junction with Swaffham Lode	8.7	(5.4)
Junction with Bottisham Lode	10.6	(6.6)
Bottisham Lock	10.9	(6.8)
Clayhithe Bridge	12.6	(7.8)
Horningsea	14.6	(9.1)
Baitsbite Lock	15.8	(9.8)
Fen Ditton	17.5	(10.9)
Chesterton Ferry	19.2	(11.9)
Jesus Green Lock	21.9	(13.6)

Headroom under Bridges

Dimmock's Cote Bridge	3.7m	(12' 2")

THE LODES

Junction with River Cam, Upware to:

	Km	(miles)
Reach Lode Lock	0.2	(0.1)
Junction with Wicken Lode	0.5	(0.3)
Junction with Reach Lode	1.4	(0.9)
Burwell Village	6.1	(3.8)

Junction of Burwell and Wicken Lode to:

	Km	(miles)
New River Drain	1.8	(1.1)
Wicken Fen	2.4	(1.5)

> **ALL DIMENSIONS MUST BE TREATED ONLY AS A GUIDE. ANY VESSEL WHOSE AIR DRAUGHT OR BEAM IS CLOSE TO A GIVEN BRIDGE HEADROOM OR LOCK WIDTH, SHOULD PROCEED WITH EXTREME CAUTION.**

The River Great Ouse

*I sing Floods muzled and the Ocean tam'd
Luxurious Rivers govern'd and reclam'd
Water with Banks confin'd as in a Gaol
Till kinder Sluces let them go on Bail.
Streams curb'd with Dammes like Bridles
taught t'obey
And run as strait, as if they saw their way.*
Samuel Fortrey (1685)

Artificial Rivers

From Denver to Cawdle Fen, 1km south of
Ely, the entire course of the River Great
Ouse – and, with one small exception, the
lower reaches of the Rivers Little Ouse and
Lark – are all artificial, that is they do not
follow the ancient natural drainage pattern.
However the rivers which made up this
pattern can be traced to this day. Remnants
still exist as small streams, ditches or lodes;
flood banks remain; parish and county
boundaries follow their course; the light-
coloured silt which they deposited as levees
forms visible tracks or ridges, known locally
as 'rodhams' or 'roddons', across the black
fens; they are marked on old maps; they are
the basis of footpaths; they are reflected in
the names of villages and old farms and
houses.

From Littleport the river, known as the
Wellstream or Old Wellenhee, flowed past
Welney, Upwell and Outwell to its outfall in
the Wash near Wisbech. It can easily be
traced today along the Old Croft River,
whose name is possibly derived from the
numerous crofts that once existed along its
route and which now forms in part the
county boundary between Cambridgeshire
and Norfolk.

The date at which the river was diverted
at Littleport to join the River Nar and flow
to the Wash at King's Lynn is not known
exactly. The route may be that of a Roman
Canal between Littleport and King's Lynn,
which was used for transport but not
drainage. A plausible explanation is that the
old canal was opened up to become a
drainage channel. Tradition however says it
was cut to drain Littleport during the floods
of 1236.

At Prickwillow the river changed
direction and ran for about 1½km in a
channel which is a part of the present River
Lark. Its course is reflected in the footpath
which goes between Tom's Hole Farm and
Folly Farm near Prickwillow to Old Bank
Farm and Further Moor's Farm near
Littleport. At Old Bank Farm it was joined
by the River Little Ouse and it is here that
there are some of the best local examples of
rodhams. At Further Moor's Farm, the
river turned towards Littleport along the
line of Holme's River.

From south of Ely, the early course of the
river was around Stuntney, along the line of
Roll's or Roller's Lode to the Old Plough,
once a riverside inn and now a private
house, where it was joined by the River
Lark. It continued parallel to and a little to
the north of Middle Fen Bank to
Prickwillow where it was joined by a small
stream which was later to become an
integral part of the present River Lark.

Many of the artificial watercourses are
themselves ancient. The diversion of the
river from Stuntney to Ely, whilst said by
some to be Roman, is more likely to be
associated with the great period of monastic
building in the 10th and 11th centuries.
After this diversion the river flowed in an
artificial cut to join the natural river near
the Old Plough. This cut became extinct
when the channel between Ely and
Littleport, known as Sandy's or Sandall's
Cut, planned and possibly started by
Vermuyden in the 17th century, was
completed in 1830.

These artificial channels all gave a more
direct route to the sea and, as they became
established, many of the old rivers and the
outfall to the Wash at Wisbech fell into
decline.

Denver Sluice

The sluice is one of the finest flood defence
and land drainage structures in the United
Kingdom. It is central not only to East
Anglia's land drainage and flood defences
but also navigation and water resources.

The first sluice was built by the Dutch
engineer Cornelius Vermuyden in 1652.
Whilst it was not a part of his original plans
for draining the fens, he decided it was
needed to prevent tidal water from flowing
up the Great Ouse towards Ely and to turn
it instead up the New Bedford River from
whence it could, if necessary, flood over
into the neighbouring washlands. It was
built as a dam but with a 7·25m-wide
waterway with fresh water doors to 'hold in
and lett goe the water as there bee occasion
and preserve the navigation from
Cambridge'. It was also claimed by some to

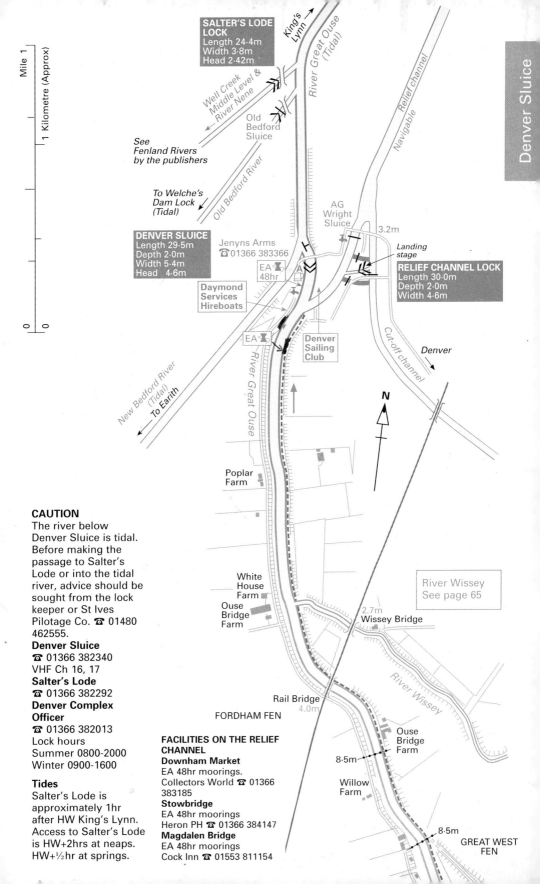

Denver Sluice

SALTER'S LODE LOCK
Length 24·4m
Width 3·8m
Head 2·42m

King's Lynn →

River Great Ouse (Tidal)

Well Creek Middle Level & River Nene ←

Old Bedford Sluice

Relief channel

Navigable

See Fenland Rivers by the publishers

Old Bedford River

To Welche's Dam Lock (Tidal)

AG Wright Sluice

3.2m

DENVER SLUICE
Length 29·5m
Depth 2·0m
Width 5·4m
Head 4·6m

Jenyns Arms
☎ 01366 383366

EA 48hr

Landing stage

RELIEF CHANNEL LOCK
Length 30·0m
Depth 2·0m
Width 4·6m

Daymond Services Hireboats

EA

Denver Sailing Club

Denver →

Cut-off channel

New Bedford River (Tidal)
To Earith ←

River Great Ouse

N

Poplar Farm

River Wissey See page 65

White House Farm

Ouse Bridge Farm

2.7m
Wissey Bridge

River Wissey

Rail Bridge
4.0m

FORDHAM FEN

Ouse Bridge Farm

8.5m

Willow Farm

8.5m

GREAT WEST FEN

CAUTION
The river below Denver Sluice is tidal. Before making the passage to Salter's Lode or into the tidal river, advice should be sought from the lock keeper or St Ives Pilotage Co. ☎ 01480 462555.
Denver Sluice
☎ 01366 382340
VHF Ch 16, 17
Salter's Lode
☎ 01366 382292
Denver Complex Officer
☎ 01366 382013
Lock hours
Summer 0800-2000
Winter 0900-1600

Tides
Salter's Lode is approximately 1hr after HW King's Lynn. Access to Salter's Lode is HW+2hrs at neaps. HW+½hr at springs.

FACILITIES ON THE RELIEF CHANNEL
Downham Market
EA 48hr moorings.
Collectors World ☎ 01366 383185
Stowbridge
EA 48hr moorings
Heron PH ☎ 01366 384147
Magdalen Bridge
EA 48hr moorings
Cock Inn ☎ 01553 811154

Mile 1

1 Kilometre (Approx)

0 0

be needed to prevent water which had flowed down the New Bedford River from Earith from entering the Great Ouse and flowing back towards Ely instead of to the sea at King's Lynn.

Within ten years of its construction there were problems – silting and, ironically, flooding. Because the tidal New Bedford River was narrower and had a bed higher than the Great Ouse, the incoming tide was held below the sluice for longer than previously and it dropped its load of silt. In summer not only was there a comparatively low flow in the New Bedford River but also the sluice would remain closed for long periods in order to hold a sufficient depth of water to enable navigation to Ely and Cambridge. There was thus insufficient flow to flush out the silt. In the winter there were often both high flows in the New Bedford River and high tides below the sluice. Consequently the water level below the sluice was frequently higher than in the Great Ouse and it was impossible to open the sluice gate to release water from the Great Ouse. This resulted in upstream flooding.

Modifications were made in 1682 but they were of little consequence. Further conflicts arose between those concerned with drainage, who wanted low water levels to accommodate the floods and the navigators who needed higher water levels. Despite many petitions from the navigators, operation of the sluice remained unchanged until its collapse in 1713 during a severe storm. It was rebuilt by a Swiss engineer, Charles Labelye in 1748–50. It was extensively repaired in 1821 and totally rebuilt to a design of Sir John Rennie in 1832. Still the arguments continued; the sluice was said to be useless for both flood protection and navigation and should be demolished.

The Denver Complex

To solve these problems, Sir Murdoch MacDonald and Partners proposed in 1940 that a 'relief channel' be built to take the flood waters from the Great Ouse above Denver directly to an outfall at St Germans near King's Lynn. However not only did the war intervene but the floods of 1947 showed that this in itself would have been insufficient to prevent the flooding which had occurred. In 1954 the scheme was revised: first, the size of the Relief Channel was to be increased and extended to join the tidal river just upstream of King's Lynn and, second, the flow in the rivers Wissey, Lark and Little Ouse was to be intercepted before crossing the fens by a 'cut-off channel' leading to Denver.

Thus in times of flood, water from the high ground to the east of the fens could either flow naturally to the Great Ouse or be intercepted by the cut-off channel and led by the relief channel straight to the sea at King's Lynn. Similarly the flow in the Great Ouse could either flow into the tidal Great Ouse at Denver or be diverted through the relief channel to King's Lynn. Whilst the flood defence standards of the fens were immediately and dramatically increased by this flexible scheme, some problems with siltation still remain.

The works were finished in 1964 and it is interesting that Vermuyden's original plans of 1640 provided for not only a 'relief channel' but also a 'cut-off channel' along virtually the same course as the modern rivers. Had they been built at that time some of the problems associated with Denver Sluice might never have arisen.

These flood defence works were to provide an unforeseen benefit to water resources. In the early 1970s two modifications were carried out at Denver. First, a sluice was built to enable water from the Great Ouse to be diverted into the cut-off channel. Second, another sluice was built to enable the natural and/or diverted water to be stored in the cut-off channel. In turn, this water can now be transferred to reservoirs some 145km away in South Essex via a new pumping station on the cut-off channel near Hockwold, and a series of other pumping stations, pipelines, tunnels, and artificial and natural watercourses. It is one of the first examples of a 'water grid' where water is transferred long distances, in this case from Buckinghamshire, Bedfordshire and Cambridgeshire to South Essex.

Whilst Denver Sluice is at the tidal limit of the River Great Ouse, there is a 17km non-tidal navigation along the Flood Relief Channel towards King's Lynn. The lock, between the Residual Flow Sluice and the Diversion Sluice, accommodates two 21m narrow boats and 48 hour moorings are available. The navigation ends at Wiggenhall Bridge.

The complex is well worth visiting and whilst there is no visitor centre, parties can be catered for at a cost and provided prior arrangements are made ☎ 01480 414581.

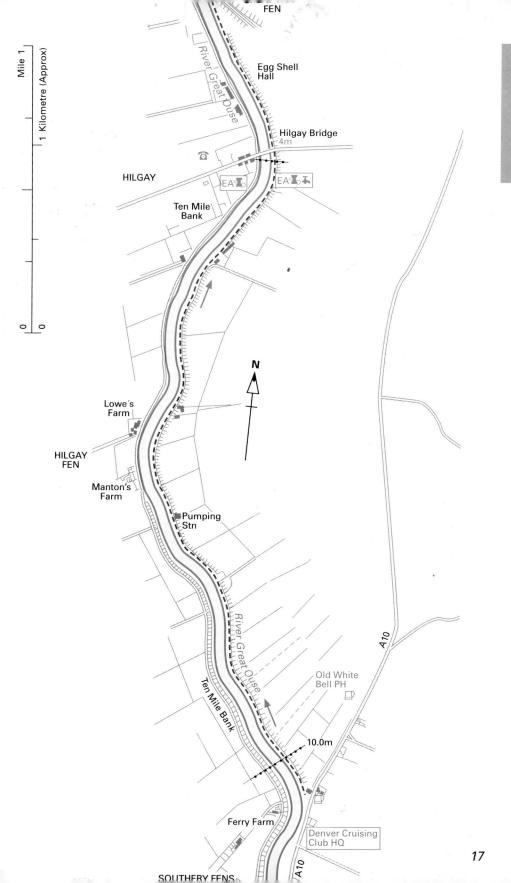

FEN

Egg Shell
Hall

River Great Ouse

Hilgay Bridge
4m

HILGAY

EA

EA

Ten Mile
Bank

Mile 1

1 Kilometre (Approx)

N

Lowe's
Farm

HILGAY
FEN

Manton's
Farm

Pumping
Stn

River Great Ouse

Ten Mile Bank

Old White
Bell PH

A10

10.0m

Ferry Farm

Denver Cruising
Club HQ

SOUTHERY FENS

A10

Denver to Southery

The first view of Denver Sluice brooding over the landscape is somewhat ominous. Here, water from Cambridge and Ely which has come down the rivers Cam and Great Ouse joins with water from Bedford and Huntingdon which has flowed down the Great Ouse to Earith and thence along the tidal New Bedford River to Denver. Together they continue as a large tidal river to outfall in the Wash at King's Lynn. A short distance downstream, Salter's Lode lock gives access to the Middle Level and in turn to the River Nene at Peterborough and the Grand Union Canal system near Northampton. The lock-keeper's advice must be sought before attempting to navigate either through the Middle Level or to King's Lynn.

On the west bank of the river are private moorings, Environment Agency moorings (with facilities for a longer stay for those waiting for suitable conditions to cross the Wash), boat hire (half-hour to weekly from Daymond Services ☎ 01366 383618) and the Jenyn's Arms which offers moorings to patrons, accommodation in the new Sluice Lodge, a restaurant and excellent bar snacks. At the complex there is a large car park, public slipway, toilet pump-out and the Denver Sailing Club.

In the village, a short distance to the east, is a particularly fine corn windmill (open during the summer from 10.00am to 4.00pm Wednesday, Saturday and Sunday). East Hall Manor with its somewhat incongruous windows was the home in 1765 of Captain George William Manby, 'Fellow of the Royal Society, Inventor and Sailor' (see River Wissey). The attractive church of St Mary is built of the local brown carstone and, whilst much restored, has a late 13th century tower and some 15th century woodwork. Further to the east, the Tudor Denver Hall, home of the Willoughby family, with its Elizabethan gatehouse, dates from around 1520.

There is a post office and store and the Bell public house.

The wide river continues upstream from Denver between high flood banks past the small St Mark's church. A minor road runs along the top of the west bank. The River Wissey joins the Great Ouse, somewhat insignificantly from the east, a short distance below an iron railway bridge carrying the King's Lynn to Ely railway line.

A little before the settlement of Ten Mile Bank is a small brick outfall of the newly restored Littleport and Downham Pumping Station. Built in 1819, it housed probably the second steam engine (30hp) to be used for fen drainage and steam was to remain until replacement by diesel engines over 100 years later in 1935. Five engraved stone plaques set in the wall commemorate the principal events in the station's history.

At Ten Mile Bank itself there are short stretches of Environment Agency moorings on each bank upsteam from the road bridge (the first since Denver) and the Windmill Inn (snacks).

For the next few kilometres until Southery and the headquarters of the Denver Cruising Club with its private moorings and motor boats, there is little of interest, indeed the local inhabitants say, "It is quite exciting to see a cow on the banks"!

Southery to Littleport

Between Southery and Littleport, the river passes through countryside which has been described as the loneliest within 100 miles of London. Its massive flood banks stand high above the vast extent of low-lying rich agricultural fenland, criss-crossed by straight roads, straight railways and straight drainage ditches. It is a hard country. In dry weather, winds can whip up soil and seeds into huge black clouds which sweep across the fen like a sandstorm, known locally as a 'fen blow'. In wet weather, pumps struggle to empty full drainage ditches into rivers which themselves are brimful and threaten the surrounding land with flooding. However whilst winters can be bitter and summers roasting, the ever-changing skyscape is magnificent.

The sizeable village of Southery is built on a fenland isle. There are few buildings of any antiquity and the medieval church of St Mary fell into ruin when the existing church was built in local carstone in 1858. As well as agricultural workshops there is a general store, post office, butcher, antique shop and the Old White Bell Inn.

Before a pumping station which drains the vast area of Southery Fen, the river turns south parallel to the A10. This bend is the site of an ancient major river crossing. In the 17th century, the road from Littleport to Southery ran along the west side of the Great Ouse to cross it here between Ferry Farm on the west and the former old riverside inn, the Ferry Boat, on the east. The crossing could even date from

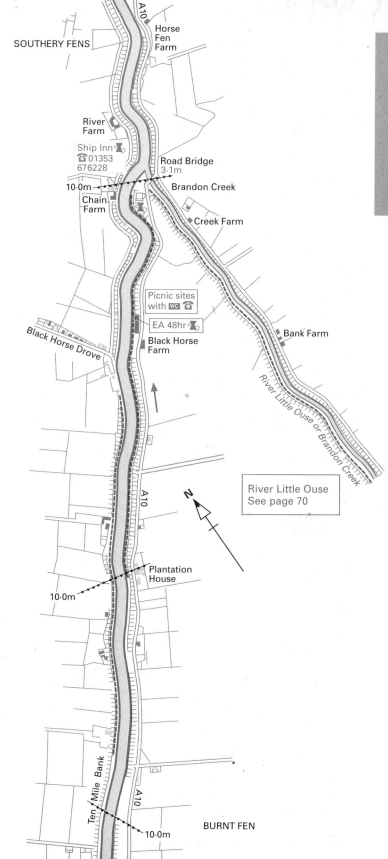

Mile 1

1 Kilometre (Approx)

0

0

SOUTHERY FENS

A10

Horse
Fen
Farm

River
Farm

Ship Inn
☎ 01353
676228

Road Bridge
3·1m

10·0m

Brandon Creek

Chain
Farm

Creek Farm

Black Horse Drove

Picnic sites
with WC ☎

EA 48hr

Black Horse
Farm

Bank Farm

River Little Ouse or Brandon Creek

A10

N

River Little Ouse
See page 70

Plantation
House

10·0m

Ten Mile Bank

A10

10·0m

BURNT FEN

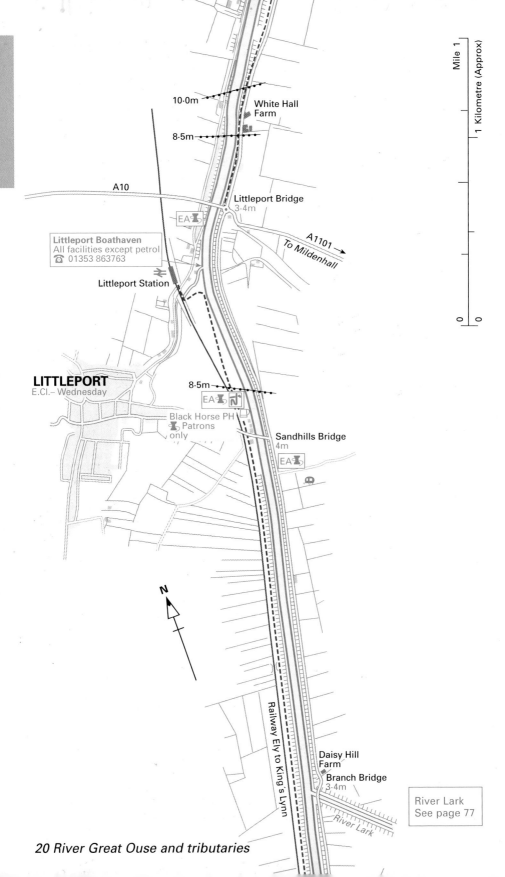

10·0m

White Hall
Farm

8·5m

A10

Littleport Bridge
3·4m

A1101 →
To Mildenhall

EA

Littleport Boathaven
All facilities except petrol
☎ 01353 863763

Littleport Station

LITTLEPORT
E.Cl.– Wednesday

8·5m

EA

Black Horse PH
Patrons
only

Sandhills Bridge
4m

EA

N

Railway Ely to King's Lynn

Daisy Hill
Farm
Branch Bridge
3·4m

River Lark

River Lark
See page 77

Mile 1

1 Kilometre (Approx)

0

0

20 River Great Ouse and tributaries

Roman times. The A10 from Southery aligns exactly with a straight drove to the west of the river and which passes Ferry and Lower Ferry Farms. This drove might in turn have led directly to the Roman road between Ely and King's Lynn which ran in a straight line between Littleport and Downham Market well to the west of the present river course.

On a bend just before the Environment Agency moorings and a picnic area sandwiched between the A10 and the river, the Little Ouse joins the Great Ouse at Brandon Creek, site of the Ship Inn (bar snacks, restaurant and moorings for patrons).

The neighbourhood is rich in folklore and legend. At the Inn, reputedly built by Dutch engineers in the 1640s, tales are told of violent, macabre killings: soldiers partly buried in the river banks were left to drown at the mercy of the rising tide; murderers were slowly strangled as the falling tide left them hanging from a noose. Some say their ghosts can be seen on misty evenings.

Here the Cambridgeshire/Norfolk county boundary crosses the river and wanders erratically across the fens to the west. From the east the Little Ouse flows in an ancient but artificial channel. Perhaps it then flowed along the line of the county boundary and the Old Crooked Drain to Welney long before the water was diverted at Littleport to King's Lynn. Certainly this mysterious region was once of significance; 17th century maps show a spot called Priest's Houses, now occupied by Chain Farm.

The river continues upstream in a southwesterly direction bordered on the east by the busy A10 and on the west by a minor road. It passes under electricity cables carried by large pylons that march, again in straight lines, across the fens, and flows under the A10 road bridge just to the north of Littleport. The Environment Agency has a stretch of moorings on the west bank between this bridge and the Littleport Boat Haven. The entrance to the Haven lies along the old natural course of the river.

Littleport to Ely

Littleport is somewhat of an enigma. Standing on a fenland isle, always close to a large river, it is surprising that the only buildings of any antiquity are the parish church of St George dating from the 14th century with a 15th century tower (and largely restored in 1857), the late 18th and early 19th century Old Turks Head Inn and one or two old coaching yards. Perhaps it became dominated by Ely and gradually fell into decline. Indeed in the 1750s it was said that it was 'as rare to see a coach in Littleport as a ship in Newmarket'. There is no doubt that the Littleport Riots of May 1816 stemmed from poverty, exploitation and starvation.

The men of Littleport, with friends from Denver and Southery, wanted to get even with one of the region's largest farmers. They gathered at the former Globe Inn and went to the local vicar, a magistrate. He agreed to some of their demands; however, later in the evening, somewhat the worse for drink, they attacked a number of houses including the vicarage. In spite of the Riot Act being read they continued on the rampage, marching to Ely with various weapons including a punt gun mounted on a wagon. They gathered outside the White Hart where magistrates not only agreed to their demands for food and work but reluctantly pardoned them all. Whilst some returned to Littleport, others went on a drunken spree breaking into shops and houses.

However at the start of the riot, help had been sought from the Home Secretary and the militia had been summoned. They rode to Littleport and on 24 May there was a battle outside the George and Dragon Inn; one rioter was killed; several were wounded; 56 arrests were made that day; 42 the next day. They were all tried in Ely on 22 June and the Chief Justice was Edward Christian, brother of Fletcher Christian of the *Bounty*. The death sentence was initially passed on 24 men. Five were subsequently hanged at Ely and 19 deported. Their memorial is in St Mary's church in Ely.

In Littleport today there are a number of shops, inns and restaurants. The Black Horse Inn is on the riverside at Sandhills Bridge (bar snacks, restaurant and moorings for patrons).

The river then crosses lower-lying, rich agricultural fenland in a dead straight line for 6km before reaching Ely. This stretch, called the Adelaide Course after a former local inn, the Queen Adelaide, is used by Cambridge University boat-race crews for training. The river is wide, the flood banks are high and the scenery is generally monotonous and featureless, the only landmark being the entrance to the River Lark on the east bank about half way between Littleport and Ely.

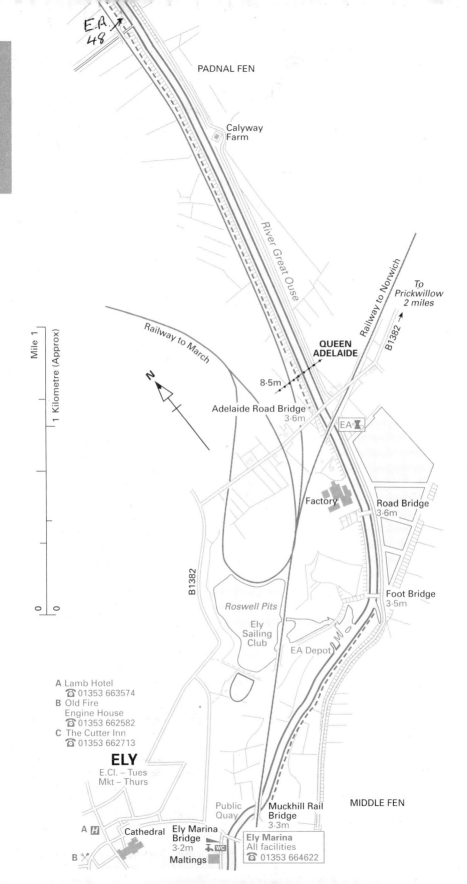

River Great Ouse

EA 48

PADNAL FEN

Calyway Farm

River Great Ouse

Railway to March

Railway to Norwich

B1382

To Prickwillow 2 miles

QUEEN ADELAIDE

8·5m

Adelaide Road Bridge 3·6m

EA

Factory

Road Bridge 3·6m

Mile 1

1 Kilometre (Approx)

N

B1382

Roswell Pits

Ely Sailing Club

EA Depot

Foot Bridge 3·5m

A Lamb Hotel
   ☎ 01353 663574
B Old Fire
   Engine House
   ☎ 01353 662582
C The Cutter Inn
   ☎ 01353 662713

ELY
E.Cl. – Tues
Mkt – Thurs

A H Cathedral

B

Public Quay

Ely Marina Bridge 3·2m

Maltings

Muckhill Rail Bridge 3·3m

Ely Marina All facilities
☎ 01353 664622

MIDDLE FEN

Immediately upstream from the road and railway bridges at Queen Adelaide are Environment Agency moorings on the east bank. Approaching Ely, the river passes a former sugar beet processing factory, currently a warehouse and distribution centre. Its old sludge pits on the east bank provide a home for much varied wild life. It then turns southwest past the entrance to Roswell Pits, home to the Ely Sailing Club and under Muckhill railway bridge, to Ely itself.

The City of Ely

'Of all the Marshland Isles, I Ely am the Queene'
Drayton, Polyolbion 21st Song

Ely – in Saxon Elig or in Latin Elge, meaning Eel Island – was described by Bede in 731 as 'the Country of Ely . . . every side encompassed with the sea or marshes'. It now stands high above the surrounding drained fenland, dominating with its great cathedral, 'The Ship of the Fens', some of the richest agricultural land in the country. Visible for miles, the sight of the cathedral, one of the most glorious and majestic buildings in England, rising above an early morning mist or an autumn fog is unforgettable.

Ely Riverside to Oliver Cromwell's House

To reach the city (early closing Tuesday) from Riverside, walk past the Maltings – built in 1868 for malting barley, with its public hall, bar and restaurant – past the former warehouse housing a large antiques centre, up Forehill to the Market Square (markets on Thursdays and Saturdays). Beyond the Almonry with shops and a tea-room in its 12th century undercroft, is the small medieval Goldsmith's Tower and Sacrist's Gate which gives access to the Cathedral precincts.

Walking parallel to the Cathedral, continue past the timber-framed Tudor Steeple Gateway towards the Palace Green flanked by fine old houses. To the south is Bishop's Alcock's Palace dating from the 15th century and in whose garden is a huge plane tree, said to be one of the largest and oldest in England. The palace is now a Sue Ryder home. The cannon on the Green was given to the city after its capture from the Russians at Sebastopol. Heading away from the Cathedral on the right is the Old Fire Engine House, now a restaurant, tea-room and art gallery. Opposite is the parish church of St Mary dating from the early 13th century and possibly standing on the site of the first religious settlement on the Isle founded in 597 by St Augustine.

Immediately to the west is the half-timbered Cromwell House, also dating from the 13th century. Allegedly haunted, it has been variously the home of Oliver Cromwell for ten years, the vicarage of St Mary's church, a pub and now, refurbished in Cromwellian style, the Tourist Information Centre.

Oliver Cromwell's House to the Riverside

Retracing the path across Palace Green, the main entrance to the Cathedral is through the great West Door. On the floor is a maze and it is said that if the path through it is straightened out it will be the same length as the height of the west tower. St Etheldreda, after two unsuccessful marriages, became a nun and in 673 founded a monastery, which some 200 years later was ransacked by the Danes. Another 100 years later the monastery was reorganised as a convent for Benedictine Monks. The present cathedral dates from 1081 and has two significant 14th century additions, the Lady Chapel with its delicate carved stonework and the octagonal Lantern Tower, built with oak pillars 19m long and nearly 1·25m wide in 1321, after the original central tower had fallen.

Whilst during the Dissolution of the Monasteries by Henry VIII, Ely suffered less than others, it did suffer at the hands of Oliver Cromwell who, whilst being Governor of the Isle of Ely and Champion of the Rights of Fenmen, in January 1644 closed it for the next 17 years. Indeed in the Lady Chapel only one statue remains complete with its head.

The Cathedral with its Norman, Early English, Decorated, Perpendicular and Post-Reformation architecture, is open for a charge to the public.

Leaving the Cathedral by the South Door past a slab bearing the poem *The Spiritual Railway*, there are on the left a number of ancient monastic buildings; part of the 13th century Monk's Infirmary now incorporated in the Deanery, the timber-framed 14th century Powcher's Hall the blood-letting house of the early monastery, the 13th

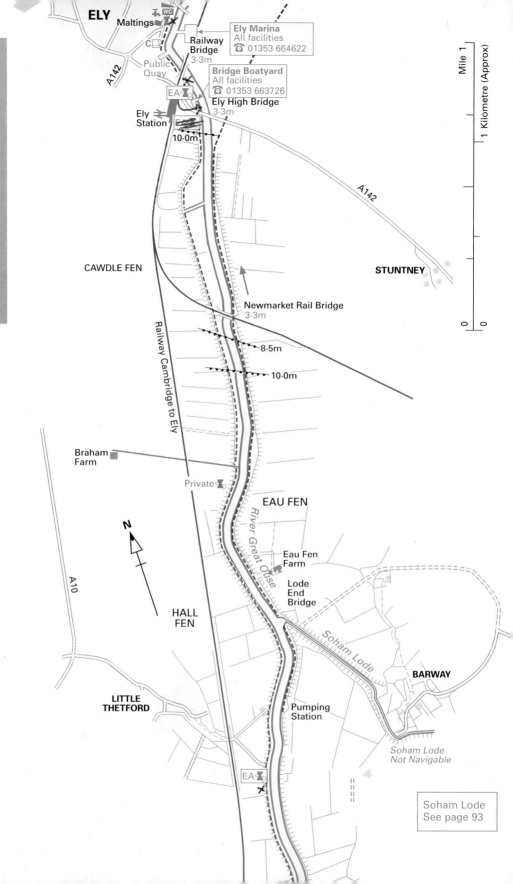

River Great Ouse and tributaries

ELY
Maltings
WC
Railway Bridge 3·3m
Public Quay
A142
C

Ely Marina
All facilities
☎ 01353 664622

Bridge Boatyard
All facilities
☎ 01353 663726
Ely High Bridge 3·3m

EA

Ely Station
EA
10·0m

CAWDLE FEN

A142

STUNTNEY

Mile 1

1 Kilometre (Approx)

Railway Cambridge to Ely

Newmarket Rail Bridge 3·3m
8·5m
10·0m

0
0

Braham Farm

Private

EAU FEN

River Great Ouse

Eau Fen Farm

Lode End Bridge

N

A10

HALL FEN

Soham Lode

BARWAY

LITTLE THETFORD

Pumping Station

Soham Lode Not Navigable

EA

Soham Lode
See page 93

century Black Hostelry accommodation for black-robed monks from other Benedictine Monasteries and the 14th century Walsingham House now a part of the King's School.

Further to the south, paths surround another cluster of ancient buildings; the 13th century Great Hall of the Monastery now the Bishop's home, the 14th century Queen's Hall said to have been built by Prior Craudon for entertaining Queen Philippa, wife of Edward III, now the King's School headmaster's house, the 12th and 14th century Prior House and Choir House, both currently used by the school, the 14th century Prior Craudon's Chapel with its wall paintings and medieval tiled floor, the 14th century Ely Porta the great South Gatehouse once used as a prison and now a part of the school and a long 14th century barn now the school's dining hall.

To return to the river, cross the Meadow to the west past the Norman motte and bailey of Ely Castle down to Broad Street. A narrow lane beside a 14th century merchant's house, the Three Blackbirds, leads to the Cutter Inn and back to Riverside.

Ely Riverside

Lying between a railway bridge to the north and the Ely High Road Bridge to the south, the Riverside at Ely, along the majority of which are 48-hour public moorings, is popular and attractive. To the north the moorings are relatively quiet and facilities for fresh water and chemical disposal are available. Facing an open area where, previously, goods were unloaded from the river, an extensive 19th century warehouse houses a large antiques centre. A short distance up Waterside towards the city centre past the antiques warehouse is a well-stocked chandlery. By a public slipway, the footbridge over the river leads to Loveys Marine, Ely Marina, which, with its large workshops, provides water, gas, petrol, diesel and, for a small fee, secure overnight moorings with full toilet facilities. The nearby Maltings, built in 1868 to process locally grown barley into malt, has been converted into a public hall, where films and concerts are regularly presented and where meals can be obtained. The Babylon Art Gallery is recommended. Opposite the well-known Cutter Inn (bar meals) are the King's School and University of Cambridge boathouses, the latter being used by the University Boat Race crews during training before the annual race against Oxford University.

Upstream from the Old Boat House Café is the railway bridge carrying a busy line linking the Midlands and the east with Cambridge and London. The Bridge Boatyard lying between the railway bridge and Ely High Bridge, has a small private marina, hire boats (weekend and longer term) and provides both water and diesel. It is generally open between Easter and the end of October.

It is a short walk to the railway station opposite which is a new Tesco superstore. In Broad Street, running parallel to Riverside, there are Indian and Chinese takeaways and a fish and chip shop.

Standing on Riverside, it is difficult to imagine nowadays that the River Great Ouse actually runs in an artificial channel as it passes close up against the City of Ely. Its earlier course was well to the east passing near to Stuntney. The origins of the present course are not clear; it is unlikely to be Roman since whilst no Roman artefacts have been recovered from the present bed, many have been found in and near the old river bed at Stuntney. It is more likely to date from the period of monastic building during the 10th and 11th centuries.

Ely to Pope's Corner

For the next 5km or so, whilst the wide river is relatively featureless as it runs between high flood banks, the area is rich in history. To the east, Stuntney rises abruptly from the fens. It was first connected to Ely by a Bronze-Age causeway lying probably to the north of the present road. According to legend its route was disclosed to St Edmund in a dream. Later this causeway became important and a Roman road passing through Stuntney and Soham connected Ely with Colchester. As well as Bronze-Age relics, traces of Roman road metalling, a Romano-British jetty and Roman pottery have been found at Stuntney. The causeway was rebuilt in the 12th century and there was a wooden bridge by the 14th century.

It is most likely that William the Conqueror launched his famous attack on Hereward the Wake in Ely from Stuntney, crossing the River Great Ouse to Braham Farm, north of Little Thetford. Certainly a number of 11th century weapons have been

recovered from the bed of the river here.
There are traces of medieval earthworks at
Braham and the distances correspond with
contemporary accounts of the battle.
Nearby land was called Herewardsbech in
the 14th century and a local river was called
the Alderbrook. Could these, as opposed to
the village of Aldreth, have given the
contemporary name of Alrehede or
Alreheche to his crossing point?

In Stuntney itself only a recently
renovated barn and earthworks remain of
the Tudor Stuntney Old Hall, once home to
Oliver Cromwell's mother and uncle. The
church of St Cross, originally Norman, was
drastically rebuilt in 1876 and 1900 with
black flint walls. There are no amenities in
the village.

Continuing south under the Newmarket
rail bridge, past a small creek on the west
leading to Braham Farm, the character of
the river begins to change subtly, perhaps
reflecting a natural rather than artificial
watercourse. Soham Lode (not navigable)
joins the river at an ugly sluice and
pumping station. After a short distance on
the west bank is a small culvert leading to
another pumping station. An inset stone
tablet with an indecipherable date
commemorates works carried out for the
Thetford Fen District under the direction of
six acting commissioners.

In the late Bronze Age there was a major
river-crossing between Barway to the east
and Little Thetford to the west. In Barway,
the 14th century church of St Nicholas has
been converted into a house. The ragstone
church of St George in Little Thetford, also
dating from the 14th century, was rebuilt in
the mid-19th century. Nearly opposite this
church is a unique red-brick thatched round
house. Whilst it might be considered to be
the base of a windmill, it is also claimed to
be a Beacon House built to warn of an
invasion during the wars with France. There
are no amenities in either village.

Whilst the flood banks hide much of the
scenery, there are frequent, beautiful views
of Ely Cathedral to the north. However the
best views across the modern, intensely
cultivated, fenland are to be had from the
seat on the west bank of the river above the
Environment Agency 48 hour moorings.
Marred only by the overhead gantries of the
railway line, they stretch from Suffolk,
towards Pope's Corner and Cambridge and
beyond Ely into Norfolk.

At Pope's Corner is the Fish and Duck
Inn (restaurant, bar meals, mooring for
patrons) and the Fish and Duck Marina.

The Old West River

Pope's Corner to Stretham

The Old West River links the two parts of
the River Great Ouse; the 'Ely' Ouse at
Pope's Corner and the 'Bedford' Ouse at
Hermitage Lock, Earith. It is a typical
fenland river running for much of its length
through peaty fenland in a narrow, winding
channel between artificially raised high
flood banks.

Its origins are something of a mystery. In
Roman times the river probably started as a
meandering stream somewhere near Twenty
Pence road bridge, flowed, as its name
implies, in a westerly direction. It was
joined by the Roman navigation canal, the
Car Dyke, and at Earith merged with the
Great Ouse which then flowed to the sea at
Wisbech.

The complete river was born when this
stream reversed its flow through an
eastward extension to the River Cam.
Whether this was a natural or artificial
process is not known, although because the
eastern part of the river is relatively straight,
it was probably artificial and possibly
medieval.

After leaving Pope's Corner and the Ely
to Cambridge railway line, the river turns in
a southwesterly direction passing under the
new road bridge at Gravel Farm, where
until the 1930s there had been a ford, and
reaches Stretham Old Engine.

The engine was built in 1831 to lift water
from some 2,500ha of fenland up into the
Old West River. The original engine was a
Boulton and Watt steam double-acting
rotating-beam engine. This drove an 11¼m
diameter scoop wheel at 4rpm, lifted 30
tonnes of water per revolution and
consumed 5 tonnes of coal per day.
Shrinkage of the surrounding fenland due to
draining necessitated a series of scoop
wheels. The first was 8·8m in diameter; this
was replaced in 1850 with one 10m in
diameter and in 1896 with the existing
11¼m diameter wheel which would now be
ineffective. Although diesel engines were
installed in 1925, the steam engine was still
working in 1941. It is now preserved,
together with all its tools and fenland relics,
in the old pump house, open to the public
from Easter to September, weekends and
bank holidays 11.30am to 5.00pm. (☎
01353 649210)

On the north bank near the bridge, is a
short stretch of Environment Agency 48-

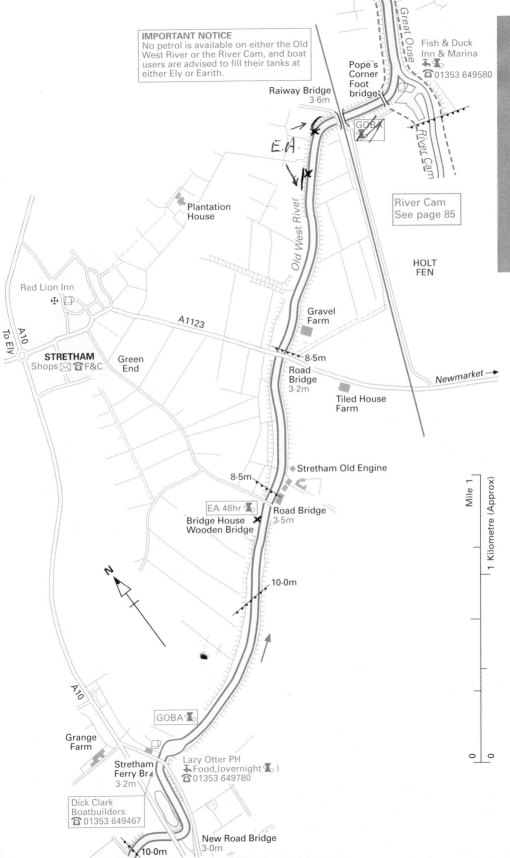

IMPORTANT NOTICE
No petrol is available on either the Old West River or the River Cam, and boat users are advised to fill their tanks at either Ely or Earith.

Great Ouse

Fish & Duck Inn & Marina
☎ 01353 649580

Pope's Corner Foot bridge

Railway Bridge 3·6m

GOBA

E.A.

River Cam

River Cam
See page 85

Old West River

Plantation House

HOLT FEN

Red Lion Inn

A1123

STRETHAM
Shops ✉ ☎ F&C

Green End

Gravel Farm

8·5m
Road Bridge 3·2m

Newmarket →

Tiled House Farm

Stretham Old Engine

8·5m

EA 48hr

Bridge House
Wooden Bridge

Road Bridge 3·5m

10·0m

N

Mile 1

1 Kilometre (Approx)

GOBA

Grange Farm

Stretham Ferry Br
3·2m

Lazy Otter PH
Food,(overnight)
☎ 01353 649780

Dick Clark Boatbuilders
☎ 01353 649467

A10
To Ely

A10

10·0m

New Road Bridge
3·0m

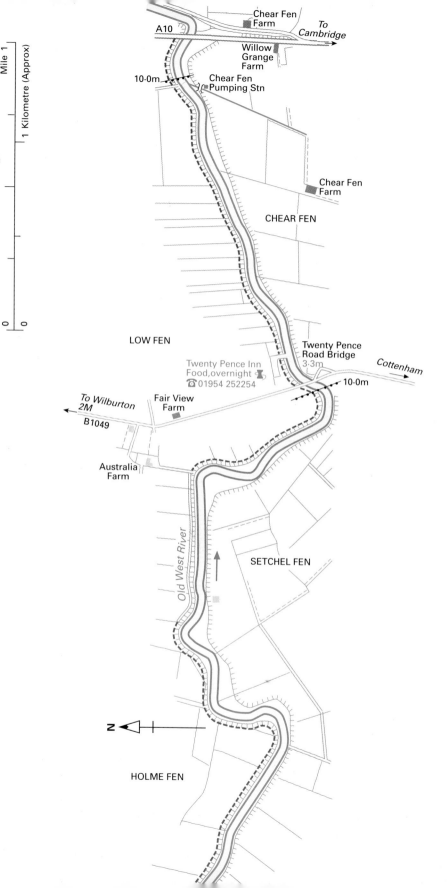

Mile 1

1 Kilometre (Approx)

0

0

Chear Fen
Farm

A10

To
Cambridge

Willow
Grange
Farm

10·0m

Chear Fen
Pumping Stn

Chear Fen
Farm

CHEAR FEN

LOW FEN

Twenty Pence
Road Bridge
3·3m

Cottenham

Twenty Pence Inn
Food, overnight
☎ 01954 252254

10·0m

To Wilburton
2M

Fair View
Farm

B1049

Australia
Farm

Old West River

SETCHEL FEN

N

HOLME FEN

hour moorings. Stretham, 1½ km to the north, has a few 17th century buildings and an early 15th century village cross. The parish church of St James, restored in 1876, retains some 12th and 14th century work. To the south, the Rectory is mainly 16th century although parts date from the 14th century. In the middle of the village the Red Lion Inn serves meals and, opposite, there is a well stocked and licensed village stores and post office. There is a fish and chip shop on the Wilburton to Wicken road.

Stretham to Aldreth

There is a short stretch of GOBA moorings before reaching the Lazy Otter public house (formerly the Royal Oak). Its attractive dining room overlooks the river and there is free mooring for patrons. In the bars is an interesting collection of local photographs taken between 1890 and 1910. The bridge was built in about 1910 on the site of an earlier bridge which in turn had replaced a ferry. Now largely redundant following realignment of the A10 trunk road, it was load tested with two traction engines. There are some sharp turns in the river between the two bridges. The marina belonging to Dick Clark Boatbuilding is private.

Care should be taken when passing the remains of some semi-derelict landing-stages on the south bank before reaching the now defunct Twenty Pence Marina and Twenty Pence Inn on the north bank. Free mooring is available for patrons and an interesting, varied selection of food is offered in the restaurant and bars which have fine panoramic views of the river and surrounding fenland.

Beyond Twenty Pence road bridge, the river starts to twist and turn reaching, after 5½ km, the Aldreth High Bridge. Here the river is crossed by Aldreth Causeway, one of three ancient causeways to the Isle of Ely, the others being at Stuntney and Earith. For centuries it was the only way between Ely and Cambridge leading across the fens from Willingham, through Belsar's Hill, a simple round early medieval earthwork, over the bridge, which has existed in some form also since early medieval times, to Aldreth. It is said that William the Conqueror took this route to Ely and that his battle against Hereward the Wake was fought near the High Bridge. Whilst this might have been one route he used, it is more likely that the main assault was made

from Stuntney where many Saxon and Norman swords have been found.

Aldreth to Earith

After a pleasant stretch between Aldreth High Bridge and Flat Bridge, where there are GOBA moorings, the river is bordered by the busy B1050 Cambridge Road before reaching Hermitage Marina where there is a small chandlery, diesel, petrol and, for a small fee, overnight moorings are available. The river then joins a short tidal stretch of the River Great Ouse at Hermitage Lock just east of Earith. This lock is the only one on the River Great Ouse network which is manned and it is operated during advertised hours.

Another of the three causeways to the Isle of Ely started at Earith, crossed the West Water and finished at Haddenham. Responsibility for the causeway and bridge belonged to the Bishops of Ely who, during the 15th century installed a hermit (whose business was to maintain the causeway and bridge) in a small hermitage on the southeast side of the river. No trace remains of either the Hermitage, after which the modern lock is named, or the adjoining small chapel dedicated to St Mary.

Before the fens were drained during the 17th century, the River Great Ouse had found its way to the sea beyond Wisbech, in part to the northwest along the complicated, meandering now extinct West Water (whose course the Huntingdonshire/Cambridgeshire county boundary roughly follows) and in part to the east, along the Old West River. The lock, which has existed in some form since the mid-17th century, now generally prevents the River Great Ouse from flowing down the Old West River and vice versa. Instead the River Great Ouse flows under the road bridge to the north immediately upstream from the lock, along the New Bedford River (Hundred Foot Drain) to the sea at King's Lynn. Navigation down this river can be difficult and hire boats are not allowed to proceed beyond the bridge. For the next ½ km upstream, the river is relatively wide but with shallows to the south near the lock.

The low-lying land to the north marks the start of the Hundred Foot Washes, bordered to the east by the New Bedford River (1651) and to the west by the Old Bedford River (1637), these being two of the principal works of the Dutch engineer

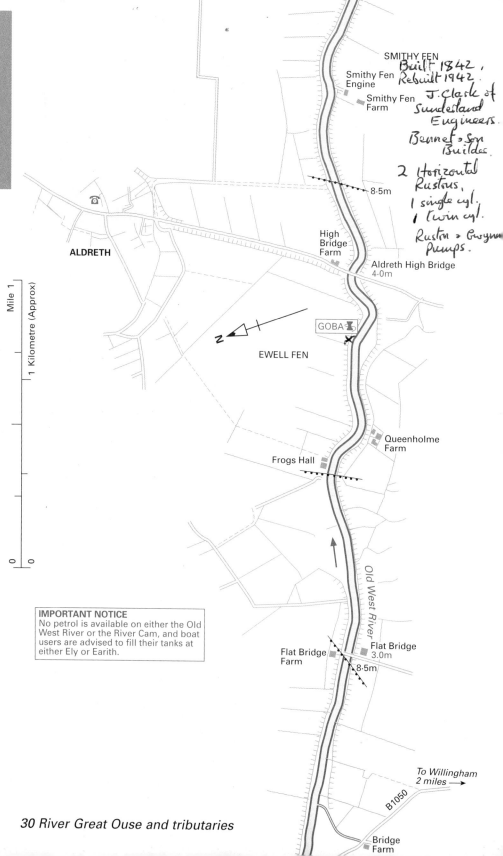

SMITHY FEN

Smithy Fen
Engine

Smithy Fen
Farm

Built 1842,
Rebuilt 1942.
J. Clark of
Sunderland
Engineers.
Bennet & Son
Builder
2 Horizontal
Rustons
1 single cyl.
1 twin cyl.
Ruston & Gwynn
Pumps.

8.5m

ALDRETH

High
Bridge
Farm

Aldreth High Bridge
4.0m

Mile 1

1 Kilometre (Approx)

EWELL FEN

GOBA

Z

Queenholme
Farm

Frogs Hall

0

0

IMPORTANT NOTICE
No petrol is available on either the Old
West River or the River Cam, and boat
users are advised to fill their tanks at
either Ely or Earith.

Old West River

Flat Bridge
Farm

Flat Bridge
3.0m

8.5m

To Willingham
2 miles →

B1050

30 River Great Ouse and tributaries

Bridge
Farm

Cornelius Vermuyden to drain the fens. In times of normal flow, water from the Great Ouse passes down the tidal New Bedford River in a straight line for 33km across the fens to Denver and thence to the sea at King's Lynn. At higher flows, water is diverted at Earith Sluice into the Old Bedford River from which it spills onto some 2,300ha of washland lying between the two rivers where it can be stored before being released back into the tidal Great Ouse near Denver.

Earthworks called the Bulwarks are situated on the Washes just to the north of the road. Whilst some suggest they are part of a line of Roman fortifications along the southern edge of the fens, their present square form with bastions at the corners dates from Cromwellian times. Earith Sluice, built in 1637 with nine holes and rebuilt in 1824 and 1954 with seven and three holes respectively, marks the eastern edge of the village. There is a memorial nearby to the crews of two RAF aircraft who died in a mid-air collision in 1942.

The Great Ouse

Earith to Brownshill

Earith, meaning a muddy landing place, is not particularly attractive when viewed from the river. Its High Street, however, contains a number of fine early 19th century houses reflecting Earith's commercial prosperity based, at that time, on the river. Of the many wharves and warehouses little now remains. However the wharf and lime kilns, where George Jewson and his son John founded the builders merchants Jewson and Sons in 1836, can still be seen in the new estate at the entrance to Westview Marina.

There are references dating from 1375 to Earith Chapel dedicated to St James; its exact site is unknown. In the mid-17th century the Quaker movement was particularly strong in Earith and a Friends Meeting House with a neighbouring graveyard was established on the site now occupied by the modern house behind and to the east of the fruit importer Minaar.

Whilst there is no public mooring, patrons can moor at the Riverview Inn (accommodation and meals) and at the Crown Inn, (meals and jazz on Sunday lunchtimes). Just upstream of the small island on the north bank of the river, boats can moor overnight for a small fee at Westview Marina which, together with Richard Allen Boat Sales, have the usual facilities including workshops, crane, chandlery and diesel fuel. In the High Street, there is a post office and licensed stores, a baker, a hairdresser and an Indian tandoori takeaway.

Bury Fen, west of Earith to the north of the river, is well known for skating, where amateur, professional and international championships have been held and where the game 'Bandy', the forerunner of ice hockey, was invented. It was also here that in 1826 a bronze Romano-Gallic statue, possibly of Emperor Commodus and presently in the British Museum, was found.

The brick piers on the river's edge mark the crossing of the former St Ives to Ely railway line and a footpath on the old embankment leads to Bluntisham and St Mary's parish church. Mainly perpendicular in style, it has a particularly interesting and rare three-sided 14th century apse. In the village there are two inns, the Prince of Wales and the Swan, a post office, a general stores and a garage.

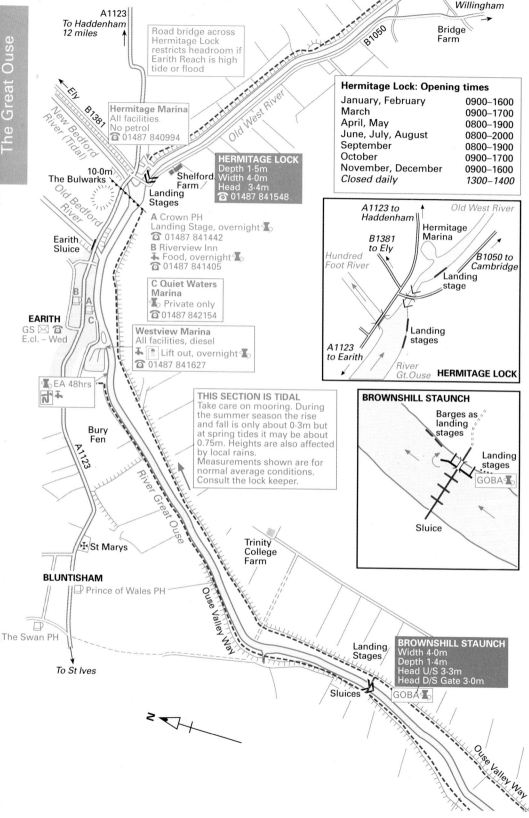

The Great Ouse

A1123
To Haddenham
12 miles

Road bridge across
Hermitage Lock
restricts headroom if
Earith Reach is high
tide or flood

Old West River

B1050

Willingham

Bridge
Farm

Ely B1381

New Bedford River (Tidal)

Hermitage Marina
All facilities
No petrol
☎ 01487 840994

Hermitage Lock: Opening times

January, February	0900–1600
March	0900–1700
April, May	0800–1900
June, July, August	0800–2000
September	0800–1900
October	0900–1700
November, December	0900–1600
Closed daily	*1300–1400*

10·0m
The Bulwarks

Old Bedford River

Shelford
Farm

HERMITAGE LOCK
Depth 1·5m
Width 4·0m
Head 3·4m
☎ 01487 841548

Landing
Stages

Earith
Sluice

A Crown PH
Landing Stage, overnight
☎ 01487 841442
B Riverview Inn
Food, overnight
☎ 01487 841405

EARITH
GS ✉ ☎
E.cl. – Wed

B
A
C

C Quiet Waters
Marina
Private only
☎ 01487 842154

Westview Marina
All facilities, diesel
Lift out, overnight
☎ 01487 841627

EA 48hrs

Bury
Fen

A1123

THIS SECTION IS TIDAL
Take care on mooring. During
the summer season the rise
and fall is only about 0·3m but
at spring tides it may be about
0.75m. Heights are also affected
by local rains.
Measurements shown are for
normal average conditions.
Consult the lock keeper.

River Great Ouse

St Marys

Trinity
College
Farm

BLUNTISHAM
Prince of Wales PH

The Swan PH

To St Ives

Ouse Valley Way

A1123 to
Haddenham

Old West River

B1381
to Ely

Hermitage
Marina

Hundred
Foot
River

B1050 to
Cambridge

Landing
stage

Landing
stages

A1123
to Earith

River
Gt.Ouse

HERMITAGE LOCK

BROWNSHILL STAUNCH

Barges as
landing
stages

Landing
stages

GOBA

Sluice

Landing
Stages

BROWNSHILL STAUNCH
Width 4·0m
Depth 1·4m
Head U/S 3·3m
Head D/S Gate 3·0m

Sluices

GOBA

N

Ouse Valley Way

Between Earith and Over in 1947 the Barrier Bank to the south of the river gave way. The winter had been very severe with deep snow. A thaw accompanied by heavy rain started on 10 March and on 13 March the rivers started to rise. During a night of gales on 16/17 March, the bank breached over a length of 50m, flooding thousands of acres of land in what was described as possibly 'the greatest flood since the fens were first drained'. The breach was finally sealed by the army on 24 March (Operation Neptune) by building a dam around the breach made of Neptune amphibious vehicles.

The river runs in a southwesterly direction from Earith with a short stretch of abandoned osier bed on the north bank, before turning south near a small pumping station, towards Brownshill Staunch. Looking northwards, there is a fine view of the former Bluntisham Rectory, a restored Queen Anne building, once the home of detective-story writer Dorothy L Sayers and into which is incorporated the doorway of the old Slepe Hall of St Ives, where Oliver Cromwell is reputed to have lived in 1631.

Brownshill to Holywell

Early staunches were simple single barriers built across a river to control water level. When left open, the upstream fords were shallow for road traffic; when closed, a depth of water could be built up and held to enable boats to navigate upstream. Passage through the single gate was relatively simple when the upstream and downstream water levels were similar. At other times it was dangerous, boats either being swept rapidly downstream by the torrent, or being slowly winched forward against it.

Brownshill Staunch dates from 1834 and today's lock has two electrically operated guillotine gates. There is no lock-keeper and the simple operation is described on the electrical panels. There is an automatic delay on each gate to prevent the lock pen from filling or emptying too rapidly. The Staunch, 62km from the sea, marks not only the tidal limit but also the eastern edge of the low-lying fenland; the high flood banks are left behind and the river begins to meander in its own wide flood plain.

The earthworks to the west surround extensive gravel workings. These extend across the river to the east via a conveyor belt at the sluice. Further development will

take place during the next 25 years. The river crosses the Greenwich Meridian shortly before reaching the Pike and Eel Inn and the Pike and Eel Marina at Overcote, where a ferry used to connect Needingworth on the west bank with Over on the east. The inn, dating from the 17th century was once patronised by Oliver Cromwell. It is now modernised and enlarged, offers accommodation and has two restaurants, one overlooking the river. There is free mooring for patrons.

Overcote Lane leads to Needingworth, about 2km from the Pike and Eel. Whilst most of the village was burnt down in 1847, some 17th and 18th century cottages and houses have survived. The most notable is the Chestnuts at the north end of the village, a large brick-built early 18th century house. Opposite is a licensed and well stocked general stores and post office. There is an old village lock-up, dated 1838, in the centre of the village, nearly opposite the Queen's Head public house.

Across the river from the Pike and Eel and where a ferry existed from the mid-16th century to about 1900, Chain Road leads to Over, also about 2km away. The village, the most populous in Cambridgeshire outside the Isle of Ely during the mid-16th century, is in two parts, Church End near the river and Over End. There are a number of fine 17th and 18th century houses in the High Street and near the church, some timbered and built of locally made red brick. Although the existence of a church is mentioned in 1178, the early church of St Mary was built in the second half of the 13th century of Barnack stone and was thatched. The present church, with its 47m high spire, reflects extensive rebuilding in the 14th century and thorough reconstruction in the 19th century. In Over End near the radio communications mast is a working windmill.

In the High Street there is a post office and general stores, a bakery and off-licence, a garage and the Admiral Vernon, a 19th century inn. The Exhibition Inn with its restaurant, is in Over End.

Immediately upstream of the entrance to the Pike and Eel Marina and on the west bank are GOBA moorings, 200m in length. The river continues in a southwesterly direction for 1½km before turning to the west and reaching, after a further 1¼km, the delightful village of Holywell. Picturesque thatched and timber-framed houses, dating from the 17th century, some

Westview Marina

High Street, Earith, Huntingdon, Cambs. PE17 3PN

Caravan and Camping
Tel. 01487 841627

Diesel and chandlery

Cranage and Repairs

Moorings

built by Dutch settlers working with Cornelius Vermuyden, line the two roads which give the village its roughly oval shape.

At the east end, where from ancient times to the 1930s there was a ferry, once used by Hereward the Wake, is the Old Ferry Boat Inn, reputedly the oldest inn in England; it is believed that liquor was sold at this spot as early as 560. The present inn, rebuilt in the 18th century and now modernised, dates from the 14th or 15th century and contains old bog-oak beams which may have formed part of an even earlier building. The inn provides accommodation, bar snacks and has a restaurant. In front are limited public moorings.

The inn is allegedly haunted. According to tradition, Juliet Tewsley, who hung herself at a nearby crossroads for the unrequited love of a local woodcutter in 1050, is said to walk each St Patrick's day, from her grave, supposedly under a slab in the floor of the public bar, to her place of death.

The village is named after the 'Holy Well' at the bottom of the hill below the church at the west end of the village. It is not actually a well but a spring, credited with healing properties and which owes its reputed sanctity to the 7th century Persian bishop, St Ivo. The surrounding brick canopy, first built in 1845 and recently rebuilt, is dressed during the annual flower festival and blessed on the Friday nearest to 24 June,

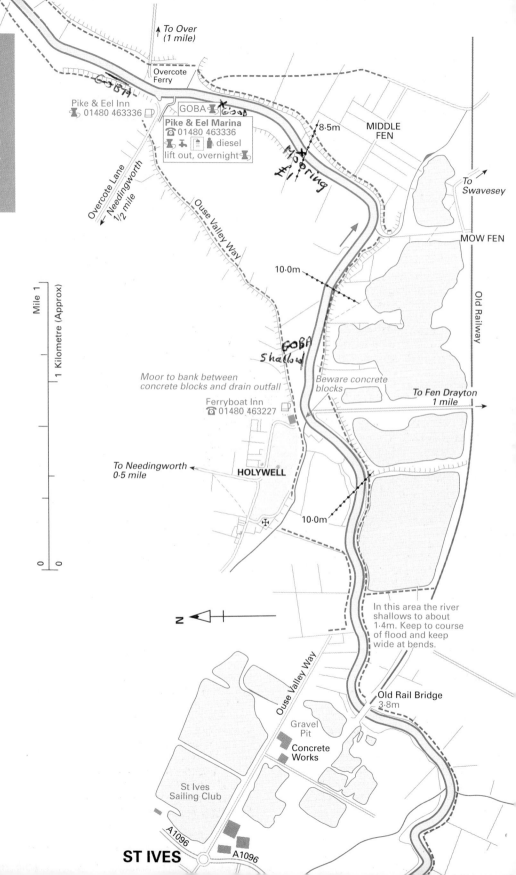

↑ To Over
(1 mile)

Overcote
Ferry

B074

Pike & Eel Inn
☎ 01480 463336

GOBA

Pike & Eel Marina
☎ 01480 463336
diesel
lift out, overnight

Mooring

8·5m

MIDDLE
FEN

To Swavesey

Overcote Lane

← Needingworth
½ mile

Ouse Valley Way

MOW FEN

Old Railway

10·0m

GOBA
Shallow

Moor to bank between
concrete blocks and drain outfall

Beware concrete
blocks

To Fen Drayton
1 mile

Ferryboat Inn
☎ 01480 463227

To Needingworth
0·5 mile

HOLYWELL

10·0m

Mile 1

1 Kilometre (Approx)

In this area the river
shallows to about
1·4m. Keep to course
of flood and keep
wide at bends.

N

Ouse Valley Way

Old Rail Bridge
3·8m

Gravel
Pit

Concrete
Works

St Ives
Sailing Club

A1096

A1096

ST IVES

the festival of St John the Baptist to whom the nearby church is dedicated. There is evidence that a church existed here in the 10th century. The present church dating from the end of the 12th century, late Norman and early transitional in style, was heavily restored in 1862 and 1915.

The river here is well known for reeds and rushes, which are gathered during July and August in flat-bottomed punts, ripened, dried and sorted before being used for thatch, chair seats and mats. The harvesting rights have been let to the same family for generations.

Holywell to St Ives

On leaving Holywell, the river shallows, meanders and narrows, reaching a pleasantly wooded stretch before passing under the bridges which used to carry the St Ives to Cambridge railway line, now closed to rail traffic and used by gravel lorries. After the bridge, the river opens up again and soon there are the first glimpses of the spires and old mills of St Ives.

About 1km from the old railway bridge, the river turns sharply through 90° and is very shallow on the inside of the bend, before turning again to a more northerly direction towards St Ives Lock. It is not manned; there is a downstream guillotine gate and a pair of upstream pointing doors.

Immediately upstream of the lock and landing stages and to the west, is the entrance to The Boathaven, L H Jones where there is a very well stocked chandlery; water, petrol and diesel are available. There are toilet facilities and overnight moorings can be arranged ☎ 01480 494040. Passing under the St Ives bypass, the wide stretch of river leads past the former old steam hosiery mill directly to the town. There is a 4-knot speed limit on the stretch of river through the town.

In the town, public mooring is available at the Town Quay on the north bank immediately before the 500 year-old bridge, through the bridge in front of the Dolphin Hotel (patrons only), at the joint Environment Agency and Dolphin Hotel moorings, upstream and to the side of the hotel and at the Waits, accessible by a small tributary upstream just past the rowing club. The water is relatively shallow at the Town Quay and The Waits. About ½km upstream on the east bank are GOBA moorings.

St Ives

St Ives, first called Slepe, the Saxon word for muddy, probably started life as a small village at the western end of the modern town. Indeed the present parish church may stand on the site of an earlier Saxon Church.

According to legend, the name St Ives is derived from the aforementioned Persian bishop, Ivo, who came to preach in East Anglia and who is said to have died near Slepe in about AD600. Some 400 years later, bones found in a field to the east of Slepe were immediately attributed by the monks of Ramsey Abbey to be those of the by-then canonised St Ivo. A priory was built on the site in 1017 and the bones removed to Ramsey. Apart from some stone walling, no trace remains of the priory which was dissolved in 1539. However, by that date, the town of St Ives had become well established between the priory to the east and the former Saxon village to the west.

The Abbey monks began to develop St Ives and a wooden bridge was built across the River Great Ouse in about 1107. In 1414 the monks agreed to a new stone bridge having six arches and which was completed in 1425. Some of the arches were replaced at the southern end in 1645 during the Civil War with a wooden drawbridge. Subsequent rebuilding did not maintain the original style; some arches are rounded, others pointed.

The chapel on the bridge is one of only three bridge chapels in the country, the others being in Yorkshire. It was consecrated in 1426 and dedicated to St Leger. Not only has it been used as a chapel but also as a toll house, an inn and a private dwelling with two additional red-brick storeys. It was completely restored in 1930, the basement being the home of the former incumbents. It is open to the public.

The Parish Church of All Saints is largely 14th and 15th century, perpendicular in style. Its elegant spire has a chequered history. It was blown down in 1741, rebuilt in 1879 and knocked down by an aeroplane in 1918. On Whit Tuesday, six boys and six girls dice for bibles under the will of Dr Robert Wilde who died in 1675. Originally play took place on the Communion Table; now it takes place on an ordinary table.

The Parish Church spire is rivalled by that of the Victorian Free Church in the Market Place. In front of this church is a fine statue commemorating Oliver

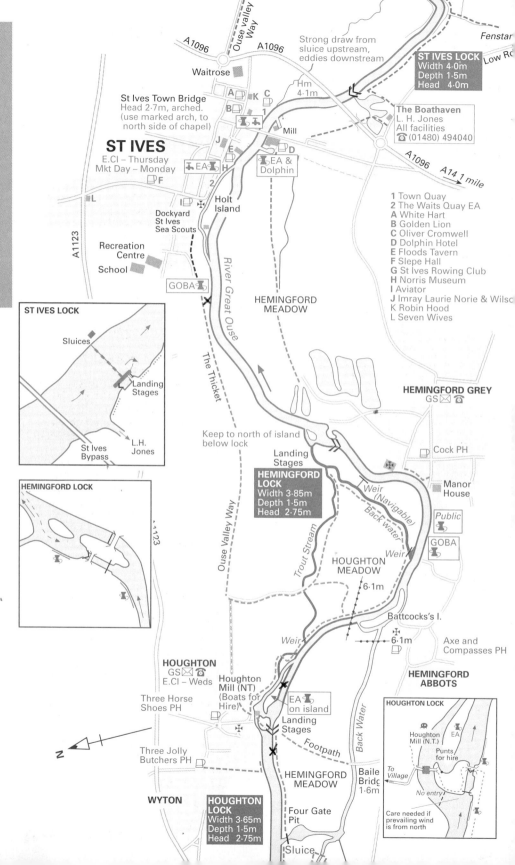

A1096
Ouse valley Way
A1096
Fenstar

Waitrose

Strong draw from
sluice upstream,
eddies downstream

ST IVES LOCK
Width 4·0m
Depth 1·5m
Head 4·0m
Low Ro

St Ives Town Bridge
Head 2·7m, arched.
(use marked arch, to
north side of chapel)

A   K   C
B
Hm
4·1m

The Boathaven
L. H. Jones
All facilities
☎ (01480) 494040

ST IVES
E.Cl – Thursday
Mkt Day – Monday

Mill

A1096   A14 1 mile

EA
F

J   E
EA &
Dolphin

EA

2

L

Holt
Island

1 Town Quay
2 The Waits Quay EA
A White Hart
B Golden Lion
C Oliver Cromwell
D Dolphin Hotel
E Floods Tavern
F Slepe Hall
G St Ives Rowing Club
H Norris Museum
I Aviator
J Imray Laurie Norie & Wilso
K Robin Hood
L Seven Wives

Dockyard
St Ives
Sea Scouts

A1123

Recreation
Centre

School

GOBA

River Great Ouse

HEMINGFORD
MEADOW

The Thicket

HEMINGFORD GREY
GS ☎

Cock PH

ST IVES LOCK

Sluices

Landing
Stages

St Ives
Bypass

L.H.
Jones

Keep to north of island
below lock

Landing
Stages

**HEMINGFORD
LOCK**
Width 3·85m
Depth 1·5m
Head 2·75m

Weir (Navigable)

Back water

Manor
House

Public

GOBA

Weir

HEMINGFORD LOCK

A1123

Ouse Valley Way

Trout Stream

HOUGHTON
MEADOW

6·1m

Battcocks's I.

6·1m

Weir

Axe and
Compasses PH

HOUGHTON
GS ☎
E.Cl – Weds

Houghton Mill (NT)
(Boats for
Hire)

**HEMINGFORD
ABBOTS**

Three Horse
Shoes PH

EA
on island

Landing
Stages

HOUGHTON LOCK

Houghton
Mill (N.T.)

EA

Punts
for hire

Footpath

Back Water

To
Village

No entry

N

Three Jolly
Butchers PH

HEMINGFORD
MEADOW

Baile
Brid
1·6m

Care needed if
prevailing wind
is from north

WYTON

**HOUGHTON
LOCK**
Width 3·65m
Depth 1·5m
Head 2·75m

Four Gate
Pit

Sluice

Cromwell who lived in the town between 1631 and 1636 in the old Slepe Hall (demolished in 1848).

Early in 1100, Henry I granted a charter for an Easter Fair and early in 1200 King John granted a second charter for a fair in October. The large Monday Market dates back to a charter granted by Edward I in 1290; there is a smaller market on Fridays.

In and around the town are five hotels, all open to non-residents. The main shopping streets are The Waits, The Broadway, Crown Street, Bridge Street and Market Hill. The principal 'High Street' banks are in Market Hill and the post office is in Crown Street. There are a number of off-licences, inns and restaurants, including Cypriot, Italian, Chinese and Indian. Fish and chips and Indian and Chinese takeaways are in The Broadway. There is a Waitrose supermarket beyond the car park at the end of Market Hill.

No trip to St Ives would be complete without visiting first the charming Norris Museum in The Waits (closed Mondays) where there is a wealth of historical and local information, and secondly J Wadsworth's off-licence opposite the museum where, among other things, there must be one of the biggest selections of whisk(e)y in East Anglia, including some malts over 50 years old.

It will take about 6 hours to make the 30km journey between Pope's Corner and St Ives. On the way a watch should be kept for seals, one semi-resident at Westview Marina and another often upstream from Brownshill Staunch. Kingfishers, warblers, cormorants, crested grebes, grey heron, coots, moorhen, redshank, Canada geese and swans (mute in the summer with, additionally, Bewick's and Whooper in the winter) can be seen frequently.

St Ives to Hemingford Abbots

Here Ouse,
slowly winding through a level plain
Of spacious meads
with cattle sprinkled o'er,
conducts the eye along
its sinuous course
Delighted.
William Cowper

One of the most attractive stretches of the River Great Ouse lies between St Ives and Huntingdon. The flood banks which dominated the lower reaches are now gone and the river meanders between low banks in a wide flood plain past the ancient villages of Hemingford Grey, Hemingford Abbots, Houghton, Wyton and Hartford.

After leaving St Ives, the river flows between the small Ingle Holt Island, a length of GOBA moorings and the wooded St Ives Thicket to the north and, on the south, the large open expanse of Hemingford Meadow to reach, in about 2km, Hemingford Lock.

The locks, weirs and backwaters between Hemingford Grey and Houghton reflect the attempted dominance of the river by mill owners and the consequent conflict with navigation. In 1618 Arnold Spencer, a local land owner and Thomas Girton, a Westminster vintner, acquired the rights to make the River Great Ouse navigable over the next 20 years. Hemingford Grey and Houghton sluices were two of a series built between 1618 and 1630 to facilitate navigation through mill weirs. Unlike staunches they were built as pound locks with two sets of doors. Navigation depended on the attitude of the millers who had first claim on the water. Sometimes they would demand a high toll for passage; at others they delayed passage for days, claiming there was insufficient water. It soon became regular practice for navigators to negotiate an agreement with the millers.

Another conflict existed between drainage and navigation and, in the 18th century, the control of Hemingford Grey and Houghton sluices was obtained by Godmanchester corporation which at the slightest sign of flooding was empowered to remove all the gates at both sluices. The task of removing these gates, which were often left removed for a very long time, was given to the miller in Godmanchester who proved, no doubt, to be a very willing ally of the mill owners at

Hemingford Grey and Houghton.

After the lock, a short, fairly narrow stretch leads round a bend to Hemingford Grey with an unforgettable view of St James' parish church perched on the river bank. Dating from the 13th century, its tower was blown down in 1741. A local legend tells how a swineherd visited a nearby company of Grey Friars who, with their Cardinal Gull'em, were feasting and drinking. He asked the Cardinal to come and give the last rites to his dying master. On entering the home the Cardinal was greeted by the Devil who said that, whilst he was pleased with what Gull'em had done, he was to damn from the pulpit all those whose views were not held by the Pope. If he did not, the Devil would visit the church and fly off with the steeple. One can only assume the Cardinal did not do as he was asked!

In the village there are two general stores, a post office and The Cock public house (pub meals). There are a number of fine houses including the former Old Rectory (1697) now a conference centre with an ancient plane tree in its garden, believed to have been planted in 1702, the early 18th century Broom Lodge with its mansard roof, the half-timbered and thatched Glebe House (1583) and the mid-18th century River House. Most notable however is the moated Manor House dating from the 11th century, making it possibly the oldest inhabited house in England. Of all the families who have lived there, two are famous.

First was the family of John Gunning, whose daughters Mary and Elizabeth were to become notorious beauties. Both were married in spring 1752, Mary to the Earl of Coventry and Elizabeth, clandestinely at midnight in Mayfair, to the Duke of Hamilton, without banns, a licence or a traditional wedding ring, the ring of a bedside curtain being used instead. The ensuing scandal resulted in Lord Hardwicke's Marriage Act of 1754. Elizabeth's second marriage was to the Duke of Argyle, so not only did she marry two dukes but she was also mother to four dukes and an earl!

More recently the Manor was home to Lucy Boston, author of the famous Green Knowe children's books. Their setting is the Manor House itself with its own unique timeless atmosphere where children and adults can feel they have entered the very special world of Green Knowe. Lucy was

not only an author: she designed and made exquisite patchwork quilts and she created a beautiful scented garden with pinks, lavenders and some 200 traditional roses all bred before 1900, forming one of the best collections in the country. The gardens which can be glimpsed and entered from the riverside are open most days of the year; tours of the house are available by appointment only ☎ 01480 463134.

A footpath goes between Hemingford Grey, past a stretch of GOBA moorings, and Hemingford Abbots which lies on a backwater of the Great Ouse behind Battcock's Island. There have been occasional settlements at 'The Hemingfords' for centuries. At Hemingford Abbots near Common Lane, the remains of a Palaeolithic/Mesolithic camp floor has been discovered whilst, on the Ridgeway Road, a Roman coffin and burial beaker was found in 1889. The coffin is now in the church but the beaker has been stolen. The settlement at Hemingford (the Ford of Hemma's People) was established in the mid-8th century. In the 10th and 11th centuries, land in the west was granted to Ramsey Abbey and the Abbots became Lords of the Manor. The land to the east gradually came under the jurisdiction of Reginald de Grey who became its Lord of the Manor.

The centre of this little village is particularly attractive. The 17th century thatched Axe and Compasses Inn (bar meals) faces 17th and 18th century cottages and a lane leading to the Manor House and St Margaret's parish church dating from the 12th century. A neighbouring modern house is supposedly haunted by a monastic ghost, affectionately known as Brother Dominic, perhaps from an earlier religious community. There are more thatched houses in Common Lane including the Old School.

Hemingford Abbots to Huntingdon

After Battcock's Island, the river meanders between Houghton and Hemingford meadows to Houghton. A mill beside the lock has been in existence for over 1,000 years. In about 970 Earldorman Aylwin, founder of Ramsey Abbey, bought a meadow and mill at Houghton and gave it to the Abbey as part of its endowment. At the Dissolution of the Monasteries in 1539 it passed to the Crown and was later sold by Charles I to the Duke of Manchester. In the early 1800s it was owned by Lady Olivier Sparrow and the Browns of Earith took over as tenants. Potto Brown, the 'village philanthropist' and a non-conformist, who it was said would resort to prayer in times of difficulty, taking his ledgers to church and telling God who owed him money, made a number of inventions to ensure the efficient running of the mill.

After the mill's closure in 1930, it was purchased by the National Trust in 1939 who leased it to the YHA until 1983. The existing building, dating in parts from the 17th century, has been restored, the water wheel re-instated and a hydro-electric turbine installed. It is open to the public during the summer, stone-ground flour from crops grown at Wimpole Hall (NT) can be purchased and there is an art gallery. Punts and rowing boats can be hired nearby and there is a caravan park adjacent.

A road from the mill leads past St Mary's parish church – parts of which date from the mid- to late 13th century – and past 17th century half-timbered buildings, restored in the 19th century. Surrounding a bust of Potto Brown is a newsagent, post office, licensed delicatessen, hairdresser, ladies' accessories shop and pub, the Three Horseshoes (bar meals).

Wyton immediately adjoins Houghton. Close by the Three Jolly Butchers pub, once a yeoman farmer's house with early 17th century wall paintings, is a lane leading to the sad and redundant church of St Margaret and All Saints dating from the early 13th century. Its graveyard is, however, maintained and contains a number of graves of airmen who had been based at RAF Wyton and were killed during the Second World War.

Although some distance from the river, RAF Wyton opened towards the end of the First World War and was the first of seven service airfields in the county. It was from Wyton that the first operational sortie of the Second World War, a reconnaissance flight over German ports in a Blenheim bomber, was made just hours into the war.

This was to set the scene for the future. The base was, for a time, the headquarters of the Pathfinder Squadron and, later, photo-reconnaissance was pioneered using V-Bombers, Nimrods and Canberras. Flying ceased in 1994 and the base is now the headquarters of RAF Logistics Command.

From Wyton, the river runs westwards in a wide channel past weirs and backwaters to the south and Daylock Marine Services to the north, where there is a small cafeteria and motor boats, canoes or rowing boats can be hired by the hour or day ☎ 01480 455898.

A little further upstream, also on the north bank, is Hartford Marina which offers a wide range of facilities including diesel, petrol, gas, a laundry, pump-out facilities, a shop (chandlery, beer, wine, food), boat sales, workshops, toilets and showers. As well as residential mooring, overnight mooring is available for a small fee and there is a caravan park ☎ 01480 454677.

Within the marina precincts are the Mill House Restaurant ☎ 01480 414311 and the 'Captain's Table' floating bar and restaurant. The restaurant and/or river trips can be booked ☎ 01480 462735.

Godmanchester Pits, opposite Hartford Marina, have been managed by a gravel company as a nature reserve since gravel extraction ceased in 1986. There is a rich variety of flora and fauna, including several species of warbler and many dragonflies.

Hartford, although now a part of Huntingdon, was once an ancient village, possibly older than both Huntingdon and Godmanchester. Stone, Iron and Bronze age traces and Saxon burials have been found; a ford was in existence in pre-Roman times. Unlike other local villages, Hartford did not belong to Ramsey Abbey; it was a Royal Manor with a mill and included the long-since-vanished Royal Forest of Sapley. Its church of All Saints, charmingly poised on the river bank, dates from the late 12th century and its churchyard was a favourite haunt of the poet Cowper.

In the village, the half-timbered Manor House is early 16th century and the red-brick Hartford House, whose lawns sweep down to the river, is early 18th century. There is a shop and two inns, the King of the Belgians and the Barley Mow, built in 1804 with stone from the former St Benet's Church of Huntingdon.

In August 1964 a hoard of 1,108 French and English coins dating between 1450 and 1503 was found near the inns. They were all in mint or near-mint condition and many were silver. Known as the Hartford Hoard, it was declared to be Treasure Trove and is now in the British Museum.

The river swings to the southwest past Hartford Meadows, the former site of the

HARTFORD MARINA

Hartford Marina is a family owned marina that puts you at the heart of the Cambridgeshire waterways on the River Great Ouse. Our friendly staff are able to provide a complete range of services that allow you to enjoy boating to the full.

Narrowboats Welcome

Family run for family enjoyment
Superbly located at the heart of the Cambridgeshire waterways on the river Great Ouse
Berthing - generous spacing and beautiful views combined with competitive rates
Boat Repairs - able to carry out all tasks for routine maintenance to major refits or repairs
Boat Sales - A well established new and used boat operation
Chandlery - everything you need for your boat and more

**Hartford Marina,
Banks End,
Huntingdon,
PE17 2AA**

**Contact Scott Deverell or Jill White on 01480 454677 or
Fax: 01480 455866
e-mail: hartford.marina@virgin.net**

Hospital of St Giles without Huntingdon founded in the 13th century and disappeared at the time of the Black Death, to reach Huntingdon.

Huntingdon

Cycles of poverty and prosperity

According to the Anglo-Saxon Chronicles, a town existed in 659. In 870 the Danes over-ran East Anglia, and Huntingdon became a Danish trading centre with an earthwork fortress, which, in 921, they abandoned in favour of a new fortress at Tempsford. Later in the same year, the Danes in East Anglia were finally defeated by King Edward the Elder who recovered the Huntingdon fortress and ordered it to be repaired and rebuilt for the protection of local inhabitants. An Anglo-Saxon mint was established in 955 and, in 1098, a Norman castle was built, possibly on the site of the former fortress.

The town's prosperity continued to go up and down. Whilst it suffered badly at the hands of King Stephen between 1135 and 1144, it prospered during the late 13th and early 14th centuries. By 1332 the old wooden bridge had been replaced by a stone one, there were 16 churches, a nunnery at Hinchingbrooke, a priory of Austin canons, a house of Austin friars, three hospitals and a Jewry.

In 1348, however, the Black Death had a particularly severe effect on the town, killing between a quarter and a half of its inhabitants. This was the start of another period of decline, which was to continue until the middle of the 16th century. The town was besieged and sacked during the Wars of the Roses in 1461 and, by 1535, only half the houses were occupied and four of the 16 churches used.

Because of its strategic position both on the river and at the centre of a road network, its fortunes changed again as it became a prosperous coaching centre and inland port. It escaped the ravages of the plague of 1665. In 1720 it was 'full of very good inns' (Defoe) and 100 years later was described by Cobbett as 'pretty, clean, unstenched'. In 1727 a private bank was established and by the early to mid-1800s there were five large coaching inns catering for all the major coach routes.

This period of prosperity was not to last. The arrival of the railway and Huntingdon station in 1850 caused the collapse of both the river and coaching trade. Peterborough became established as the major railway town. By 1931 the population had dropped to a little over 4000.

Yet by 1982, following the Town Development Acts of 1952, the population had increased nearly fourfold catering largely for GLC overspill. Unfortunately, 20th century development with its modern frontages, precincts, car parks, shops, building societies, banks and estate agents has caused irreparable damage to the fine Georgian façades that once lined the streets. The centre has been pedestrianised and the traffic flow on the ring road which once imprisoned the town has been improved. Now the A14 trunk road on its high embankments and viaducts dominates the landscape and there is a ceaseless roar of traffic passing by and over the county town of the former county of Huntingdonshire.

Daylock Marine Services
☎ 01480 455898

Hartford Marina
All facilities
☎ 01480 454677

The Rhymers
Weir

A

B

Bridge

GODMANCHESTER EASTSIDE COMMON

Weir

Old gravel pits (Fishing lakes)

A1123

141

HARTFORD
GS ✉ ☎

C

D

River Great Ouse

WESTSIDE COMMON

Cook's Backwater

Ouse Valley Way

GODMANCHESTER LOCK

To Godmanchester

To Brampton

Landing stage

To Huntingdon

To Brampton

Landing stage

A Captain's Table ☎ 01480 462735
B Millhouse Restaurant ☎ 01480 414311
C Barley Mow
D King of the Belgians
E Sun
F Old Bridge Hotel ☎ 01480 452681
G The George Hotel ☎ 01480 432444
H Black Bull
J Royal Oak
K White Hart
L Exhibition
M Chinese Bridge Restaurant ☎ 01480 450354
N Victoria
P Waterloo

N

A14 To Cambridge 14M

Cricket Ground

K

L

GODMANCHESTER
GS, Butchers ✉ ☎

J

Huntingdon Boat Club
☎ 01480 456963

Huntingdon Marine & Leisure
☎ 01480 413517

Huntingdon Boathaven
☎ 01480 411977

E

Purvis Marine Boat Hire
☎ 01480 453628

24hr

H

M

10·0m

EA

Landing Stage

Sainsburys

N

P

F

Shallows to 0·75m.
Keep wide at bends

HUNTINGDON
E.Cl – Weds
Mkt– Saturday

High St

Bus Stn

GODMANCHESTER LOCK
Width 4·0m
Depth 1·05m
Head 2·9m

PORT HOLME

G

Ouse Valley Way

Mile 1

1 Kilometre (Approx)

A14 Road Bridge
Head 5·5m

Huntingdon Bridge
Head 3·4m
Use eastern arch

Huntingdon Boathaven
All facilities except fuel

Huntingdon Marine & Leisure
Boat Hire

Police Stn

A1 North

A14

B1541

Huntingdon Stn

Railway

Rail Bridge
4·8m

London

Peterboro

Police HQ

Nuns Bridge

Hospital

Hinchingbrooke House (school)

Huntingdon on foot

Huntingdon is readily accessible by road, rail or river. The town offers a full range of facilities including a cinema. The Tourist Information Office is in the public library near Market Hill. There are public moorings at the Riverside Park and patrons can moor at the Old Bridge Hotel. Day boats can be hired from Purvis Marine ☎ 01480 453628 and Huntingdon Marine and Leisure which has a chandlery, provides fuel and, for a small fee, moorings ☎ 01480 413517. There is a public slipway downstream of Purvis Marine.

Huntingdon High Street starts at the stone bridge joining Huntingdon with Godmanchester. Built in 1332, it was apparently started from both sides of the river. The two parts did not meet exactly and there is a slight bend near the central pier. No trace remains of the Chapel of St Thomas of Canterbury (later to be turned into two shops) on the downstream side of the bridge. During the Civil War, the fourth arch from the Huntingdon side was removed and replaced with a drawbridge.

After the ivy-clad Old Bridge Hotel, parts of which date from the 18th century, the High Street is bisected by the modern ring road. However, before continuing along the High Street, Huntingdon Castle can be reached by following the ring road westwards for a short distance past the main entrance to the hotel. The Norman castle was destroyed in 1172 and all that remains now are the massive earthworks, split in two in 1847 by the Huntingdon-to-Cambridge railway line.

Shortly after crossing the ring road to rejoin the High Street, a small archway on the east side leads into Orchard Lane. On the left was the Old County Jail and the iron-barred windows at pavement level once lit the condemned cell. The lane here was the prison yard and the house opposite the jail also has barred windows which not only protected the inhabitants but prevented prisoners from escaping.

The next stretch has been relatively untouched by modern development and there are a number of 17th century houses. On the same side as the Methodist Church

is Castle Hill House, dating from 1787. Now offices of Huntingdonshire District Council, during the war it was the headquarters of the RAF's Pathfinder Squadron. Almost opposite is St Mary's Church, one of two churches remaining from the original 16. Although almost completely rebuilt in the 13th century with some further rebuilding in the early 17th century following the partial collapse of the tower, the original church dates from the 10th century. Inside, a plaque near the pulpit is inscribed with the name R Cromwell (Robert Cromwell, Oliver Cromwell's father).

Before the High Street becomes pedestrianised Cowper House can be found. Home of the poet William Cowper from 1765 to 1767, its 18th century façade hides a 16th century wooden-frame interior with contemporary wall paintings and beautiful plasterwork.

In the pedestrianised part of the High Street are the usual high-street shops, cafés and stores; there is little of architectural interest until Market Hill which is surrounded by some of the town's best remaining buildings. To the east, above Woolworths, is the early 18th century upper façade of the former Fountain Hotel and, next door, was the town's first private bank of 1727. To the south is the red-brick Town Hall, built in 1745 and containing two early 19th century law courts. The Falcon Inn, an old coaching inn used for a time by Oliver Cromwell as his Civil War headquarters stands next to late 17th and early 19th century houses, Walden House and Wykeham House, now council offices.

All Saints Church, probably standing on the site of an early Minster, dates mainly from the late 15th and early 16th centuries with some Norman remains. Its register contains the birth entry of Oliver Cromwell in 1599.

Fronting the High Street, opposite All Saints, is a small stone building once part of the Infirmary and the only remaining part of the Hospital of St John the Baptist founded in 1160 by David, Earl of Huntingdon. In about 1565 whilst most of the Hospital was destroyed, this building was converted to the Huntingdon Free School with two floors for the upper and lower schools respectively. Here, both Oliver Cromwell and Samuel Pepys received their early education. The building is now home to the Cromwell Museum and is the only public museum devoted specifically to Oliver Cromwell. It is open daily except on Mondays and bank holidays ☎ 01480 425830 for times.

After the pedestrianised street comes the former coaching inn, the George Hotel. Although badly damaged by fire in 1865, it has a 17th century galleried courtyard in which performances of Shakespeare are given in the summer ('Shakespeare at the George'). Between a number of insurance brokers and estate agents is the churchyard of the former church of St John the Baptist. It is adjoined by two red-brick 18th century houses.

Opposite is the private Cromwell Clinic. The present house, built in the early 1800s is on the site of the former House of the Austin Friars, first recorded here in 1258. It was demolished during the dissolution of the monasteries. However the Prior House remained and it was here in 1599 that Oliver Cromwell was born. He continued to live in Huntingdon until 1631 when he left for St Ives, Ely and London.

After a short distance the High Street is crossed again by the ring road before leaving Huntingdon for the north.

On the way back to the river, it is worth turning down Hartford Road opposite Cowper House and taking the second turn on the right which leads into Victoria Square, a pleasant small green with lime trees and the whitewashed Victoria Inn (bar meals).

Huntingdon to Brampton

Leaving Huntingdon and moving upstream, the River Great Ouse flows under the small 14th century stone town bridge, dwarfed by a massive 20th century concrete bridge carrying the A14 trunk road. On the north bank, sandwiched between the two bridges, are the Old Bridge Hotel (Garden restaurant, dining-room, accommodation, mooring for patrons) and the remaining earthworks of Huntingdon Castle. Huntingdon Marine and Leisure, where traditional mahogany punts are made, is opposite on the south bank (fuel, chandlery, day boat hire, moorings). The river turns south at its confluence with the Alconbury Brook past Huntingdon Boathaven (private moorings) towards Godmanchester.

Opposite Godmanchester to the west is Port Holme Meadow. It is actually an Island and is claimed to be the largest meadow in England (104ha). First mentioned in 1205, it has been used for a number of 'sports' including cock fighting, horse racing and flying. Today it is crossed by footpaths going between Huntingdon, Brampton and Godmanchester Lock and amongst the meadow plants, Marsh Dandelion, Brown Sedge, Great Burnett and Snakes Head Fritillary can be found.

Godmanchester Lock was one of a series built between 1618 and 1630 to facilitate navigation past the mill weirs by Arnold Spencer who had acquired the rights to make the Ouse navigable. Navigation depended on the attitude of the millers who had first claim to the water. Sometimes they demanded a high toll for passage, sometimes they delayed passage for days claiming there was insufficient water. In the 18th century Godmanchester Corporation gained control of Godmanchester lock and a local miller was given the responsibility of removing all the flood gates at the slightest sign of flooding to replace them only when the threat had receded.

This conflict between navigation and drainage was to continue. In the 1890s navigation was in decay and a stockbroker, Leonard Simpson, bought the rights and started to improve navigation to Bedford. In 1894, faced with a large flood, Godmanchester Corporation opened the sluice gates, two of which were subsequently damaged. In a following High Court action it was ruled that the Corporation had the right to open the gates. Unhappy with the Court's findings, Simpson decided to close navigation by sinking barges in front of the gates which he also padlocked shut. The House of Lords then decided he had the right to close the gates and because of this difference of opinions, the need for public control of navigation was recognised.

The main stream to Godmanchester Lock keeps to the west passing on the east a number of former mill races. At the lock with its pointing doors and manually operated guillotine gate, the upstream and downstream landing stages are on the west bank and 48 hour mooring is available on the old lock walls adjacent to the new lock. There are footpaths to Huntingdon, Brampton and Godmanchester. Immediately downstream of the lock on the east, a backwater leads past the gardens of elegant Georgian Houses to Godmanchester. There is a short length of mooring between two white posts on the north bank and a very limited length just beyond the Chinese Bridge.

A visit to Godmanchester is rewarding. It is arguably the oldest town in the county, possibly dating from a Neolithic settlement of farmers developing the light river soils and gravels. However whilst traces of Bronze Age ring ditches and Iron Age farms have been found nearby, its principal development was during the Roman Occupation starting with the construction of a military fort and the end of a Roman road running from Sandy, near a ford across the Great Ouse and close to the present Black Bull Public House. A civilian settlement soon became established, moved a little to the south and prospered during the first to third-centuries. Roads radiated out, Ermine Street to London and York and Via Devana to Cambridge and a bridge replaced the ford. A town hall, a guest house for Imperial Couriers, bath houses, temples, kilns and town walls were built.

The Anglo Saxons gave it its name Godmund's Caester after the ruins which they found. At the time of the Norman Conquest it was an estate owned by Saxon Kings, after which it thrived as a market town with a rare form of self government later to be confirmed by King John in a charter of 1212. There were common rights, inhabitants were free-men and not allowed to sell or give away their land, which according to an unusual custom descended to the youngest son of the first wife and sons and daughters who were born in the town and continued to live there became free-men and women at the age of 21.

The town continued to prosper throughout the 16th, 17th and 18th centuries within an area around which the streets roughly follow the line of the roman walls and date from the late Saxon period. The first school was started in the 14th century and was established by Letters Patent in 1561 by Queen Elizabeth. Above the doorway of the restored school is a plaque with the inscription 'Eliz. Reg. Hujus Scholae Fundatrix'. There were cattle and horse fairs, tanning works, iron foundries, brick kilns, flour mills, a brewery and a hosiery mill. It was however considered, because of its low lying position close to the river, to be the most unhealthy town in the county; Typhoid was not uncommon even in the 19th century.

A church was first mentioned in 969 and the Parish Church of St Mary, standing outside the circle of the old walls and surrounded by Roman Cemeteries, may be on the site of a Romano-Christian church. Said to be the largest church in the County, the present church dates from the 13th century. Its tower was rebuilt in 1623, paid for by local taxes, those who did not pay being imprisoned. On the south side of the chancel is a very rare Mass Dial which tells the time, starting at 0600, in Saxon 'Tides', each 'Tide' being 90 minutes. The church has its macabre side. A vicar was murdered by the towns people in the 14th century and in the grave yard is a replica memorial to Mary Anne Weems. Following a courtship which lead to a compulsory marriage, she was lured away by her husband and murdered near Royston. He was caught, tried and executed in Cambridge, hence the warning epitaph 'Ere crime you perpetrate, survey this stone . . .'

The present town owes much to its past. Whilst there is no market place or main street, there are a number of very picturesque early 17 century timber framed houses, fine 18th century merchants houses including Farm Hall with its tree-lined reflecting pool and Island Hall with its formal gardens and ornamental gardens (open to the public on Sundays in July), a 'Chinese' or 'Willow Pattern' bridge, first built in 1827 and twice rebuilt and back-waters with charming boathouses. There are tea-rooms, restaurants (English, Chinese, Tandoori), a number of shops (including an off-licence, a small supermarket, clothes shops, a bookshop), bakers, butchers, a post office and a chemist. Amongst the pubs are the Royal Oak, fronting the river and at the start of the causeway back to Huntingdon, first built in c1300 and rebuilt by Robert

HUNTINGDON
Station

Hinchingbrooke House (school)

Nuns Bridge

Alconbury Brook

PORT HOLME

Hinchingbrooke Country Park

B1514

Ouse Valley Way

EA Offices

GOBA

Rail Bridge
4·8m

BRAMPTON
GS ✉ Butchers ☎ F&C

Caravan Park

Olde Mill
Pub & restaurant
☎ 01480 459758

Pepy's House

Weir

Navigation Channel

BRAMPTON LOCK
Width 3·4m
Head 2·8m
Depth 1·48m

□ Black Bull PH

The Dragoon PH

BRAMPTON LOCK

Weir

To Brampton

Chain

Landing stage

Lock Channel

Brampton RAF

Garden Centre

Weir

Golf Course

Landing stage

To Offord

N

Mile 1

1 Kilometre (Approx)

10·0m

GOBA

Mailers Meadow

0 0

OFFORD LOCK

To Carters Boat Yard

To Brampton

To Buckden

GOBA

Landing stage

To Offord

B1043

Landing stage

Shoal

Weir

To St. Neots

Buckden Marina
All facilities
☎ 01480 810355

To Buckden 1 mile

OFFORD LOCK
Width 3·4m
Depth 1·2m
Head 2·5m

Mill

GOBA

Swan PH

OFFORD CLUNY
GS ✉ ☎

Weir

Weir

□ Horseshoe PH

Cooke after he was nearly drowned there in 1637, the Black Bull.

Leaving Godmanchester Lock, the Great Ouse turns to the west, flows under the main East Coast railway line to Brampton. However before reaching Brampton, Hinchingbrooke House can be seen to the north. Initially a Benedictine Nunnery, said to have been moved on the 12th century by William the Conqueror, the Norman buildings were almost entirely rebuilt as a mansion after the Dissolution of the Monasteries. It was to be inhabited in turn by the Cromwells, who are said to have removed the gateway from Ramsey Abbey to Hinchingbrooke in honour of a visit by Queen Elizabeth, and the Montagues, later to become the Earls of Sandwich and who lived there for over 300 years. During the late 1960s it was converted and became in 1970 the Upper School of Hinchingbrooke School. The green school uniform is the consequence of an amalgamation in 1895 between Huntingdon Free School and Waldens Charity School whose pupils, following a bequest, had green coats.

Brampton to Offord

Returning to the river, the main channel flows past GOBA moorings, private moorings and Brampton Mill, the only mill remaining of four and now a restaurant and bar (moorings available), to Brampton Lock where there has been a lock to enable navigation past the mills since about 1620. On the west bank of the river the Ouse Valley Way footpath from Huntingdon crosses Bromholme Lane, runs beside the Willows Caravan Park and through a wood to continue along the river-bank to Offord and St Neots.

A footpath leads from Brampton Mill to Brampton via Pepys' House and the Parish Church of St Mary the Virgin. Although the diarist Samuel Pepys was born in London, he attended the Free School in Huntingdon with Oliver Cromwell and lived for a short time with his parents in Brampton. It is said that he buried some money in the garden fearing either a Dutch invasion or the Plague and indeed a pot of silver coins was discovered there in about 1842. Viewing of the house, parts of which date from the mid 16 century, is by appointment only. Pepys' parents are buried in the church, which although mentioned in Domesday, has no part earlier than 14th century. Inside the

restored church are three mid-14th-century oak stalls with deeply moulded and carved misericords depicting pastimes such as carpentry, writing, weaving and harvest making.

Opposite the church is the former Manor House, now a Cheshire Home, rebuilt to an old design in 1873 supposedly on the site of an ancient Royal residence where Kings Henry 1, Henry 2, John and Henry 3 are believed to have stayed before it was destroyed by floods in 1348.

The High Street leads west through the village to the small Green edged by a chapel, cottages marked with the letters 'OBS', the Harrier Public House and Lady Sparrows School. Lady Olivia Bernard Sparrow lived at Brampton Park on the site of 12th and 13th-century houses in a mid-17th-century house which she had had rebuilt in 1820. She took much temporal and spiritual interest in her tenants, rebuilding their houses, donating a village school, and founding a hospital for the elderly in a house with an eight sided chimney in the High Street. Before her house was burnt down in 1907, it had become an Institution for the Care of Stammerers. Today Brampton Park is home to the RAF.

In the village there are some timber framed houses in the High Street. Other public houses include The Dragoon and the early 17th century Black Bull, whose beer delighted Pepys and was said by him to have 'had just a touch of wormwood'. There are several shops including a large garden centre, picture gallery, fish bar, bakery and tea room, chemist, grocery and off-licence, butcher, Chinese takeaway and a post office.

After the lock, continuing upstream in a southerly direction, the relatively wide river flows through pleasant open countryside, past a lane leading back to Brampton on the west, a weir on the east and the former Huntingdon to Kettering railway line to reach after about 2km a length of GOBA moorings on the west bank immediately downstream of a small tributary draining a number of former gravel pits. After a further 1·5km, on a series of bends, is the entrance to Buckden Marina and Watermark Club. Here the Ouse Valley Way leaves the riverside, passes through the marina, crosses the Buckden Road and rejoins the river south of Offord Lock.

The facilities at the large Marina with its wooden chalets and lodges are extensive

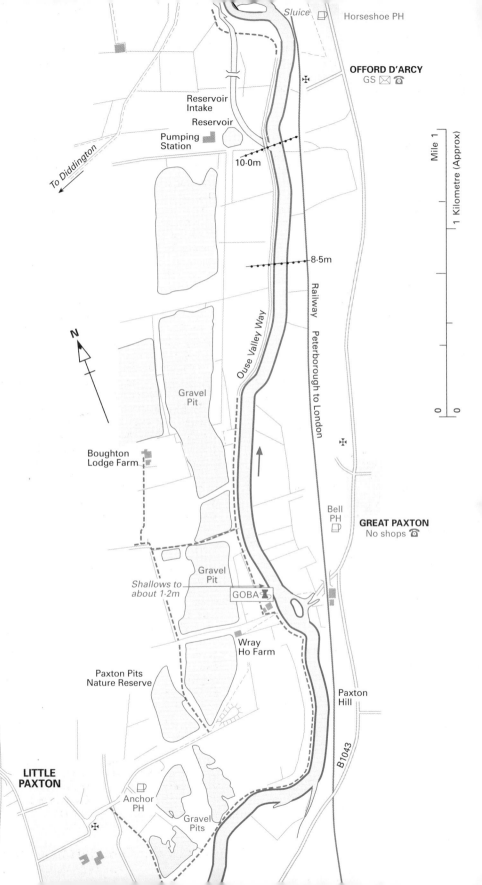

The Great Ouse

Sluice   Horseshoe PH

OFFORD D'ARCY
GS ✉ ☎

Reservoir
Intake

Reservoir

Pumping
Station

To Diddington

10·0m

8·5m

Railway   Peterborough to London

Ouse Valley Way

N

Gravel
Pit

Boughton
Lodge Farm

Bell
PH

GREAT PAXTON
No shops ☎

Gravel
Pit

*Shallows to
about 1·2m*

GOBA

Wray
Ho Farm

Paxton Pits
Nature Reserve

Paxton
Hill

B1043

**LITTLE
PAXTON**

Anchor
PH

Gravel
Pits

A1

Mile 1

1 Kilometre (Approx)

0   0

and include moorings, petrol and diesel, sewage pump out, a bar and brasserie and a leisure club with a swimming pool and gymnasium ☎ 01480 810355. A short distance upstream from the Marina entrance, a mill race joins the river from the east whilst the main channel flows between another length of GOBA moorings and the entrance to Carter's Boatyard, to Offord Lock. The Boatyard offers chandlery, gas, a slipway, a workshop and moorings ☎ 01480 811503. The road immediately before the lock goes between Offord Cluny and Offord Darcy close by on the east bank of the river and Buckden, some 2·5km to the west.

Offord Cluny derives its name from Cluny Abbey in Burgundy and to which it had been granted before Domesday. Although somewhat dominated by the main East Coast railway line which lies very close to the river for the next 5km, there are some attractive houses including an early 18th century red brick manor house, the old Swan Public House (bar meals), Manor Farm dating from the late 16th century and several thatched cottages. There is a post office and stores. All Saints parish church, although mainly 18th century has some 13th century remains, a 15th century tower and carved figures in the nave roof.

Offord Darcy (a corruption of Daney) adjoins Offord Cluny. The timber framed Horseshoe Public House dates from 1626. The redundant church of St Peter and the Manor House are a short distance from the village next to the railway line. The church is 13th century with 14th century additions. Inside are two early brasses, one on the wall to Sir Laurence Pabenham, the other on the floor to Dr. William Taylard in academic costume (key in village shop). The Manor House, originally early 17th century was substantially rebuilt in the 18th century; the house appears to have three stories but the top windows are false; there is nothing behind them.

Although it is some distance from the river a visit to Buckden is rewarding for its buildings, shops, hotels and inns. Since before Domesday, the Manor of Buckden (Bugden) had been held by the Diocese of Lincoln, the largest diocese in medieval England. To ease travel around its lands a number of palaces were built, one of which was at Buckden. Whilst there was probably a residence for Bishops in 1066, by the middle of the 12th century there was a house which was rebuilt and extended in the early 13th century to form a moated palace and court. It was burnt down in 1291 and immediately rebuilt, the fine red brick tower being added in the late 15th century. By about 1600 it had fallen into disrepair but it was restored on a smaller scale in 1660 and remained the property of Lincoln until 1870, the last bishop having left in 1837. Those who have stayed there include Henry III, Edward I, Catherine of Aragon, Henry VIII, Catherine Howard, and the Prince Regent.

In 1957 it was bought by the Catholic Church. It is used by the Order of Claretian Missionaries and is being restored as a Centre for Youth, only the original gatehouse and tower remaining. The modern church and court-yard are open to the public and guided tours can be arranged by appointment ☎ 01480 810344.

The secular interests in Buckden arose through its coaching inns, notably the George (17th and 18th century) and opposite the older Lion Hotel. With its fine wooden carved beams and ceiling boss, it may once have been a guest house for lesser visitors to the Palace. The Manor House opposite the parish church of St Mary, restored but with some 13th and 15th century stonework and where angels with books and musical instruments look down from the roof, is partly medieval with 16th, 17th and 18th century additions. In the village today are two further inns, the Vine and the Spread Eagle, a number of fashion shops, a news agent, and a post office, stores and off-licence.

The Offords to St Neots

Leaving Offord Lock, the navigation channel turns sharply to the east and then back to the south returning to its wide natural course before passing the river water intake for Anglian Water's Grafham Water Reservoir some 6·5km away. To begin with the river runs through generally open agricultural land albeit bordered on the east by the high speed East Coast main railway line. However after about 2km approaching Great Paxton, behind a number of private moorings on the west, there is an extensive area stretching to Little Paxton of worked out gravel pits, now managed as nature reserves and for recreation. The Ouse Valley Way, which rejoined the west river bank upstream of Offord Lock, passes between these pits and the river.

ST. NEOTS PAPER MILLS LOCK

To Little Paxton

To Offord

Landing stage

Landing stage

L.S.

To St.Neots

LITTLE PAXTON

B1041

Gravel pit

Shallow about 1.0m

6·1m

Sewage Works

Huntingdon

6·1m

ST NEOTS LOCK
Width 3·3m
Head 3·75m
Depth 1·05m

Factory Bridge
Head 3·9m

Sluices
Road Bridge
2·9m

10·0m

Shallows to about 0·7m

Priory Hill Park

Navigable for small cruisers for about 1mile

River Kym

Ouse Valley Way

Island Common

N

B1041

B1043

St Neots Station

Crosshall Marina
All facilities – no petrol
☎ 01480 472763

Lammas Meadow

To Cambridge 17 miles

Golf Course

Ouse Valley River Club

B1048

A The Bridge House Beefeater
B Old Falcon PH
C St Neots Rowing Club

Priory Centre
Good

C

A

ST NEOTS

B1428

St Neots Bridge
2·8m

B

Hen Brook

St Neots Marina
All facilities – no petrol
☎ 01480 472411

EATON FORD

Council Moorings

Riverside Park

Slope

EA

Not

Footbridge

EYNESBURY

Railway London – Peterborough

EATON SOCON LOCK

To St. Neots

To Eaton Socon

River Mill Boats Tavern, tea room and gallery

B1043

Weir

To Tempsford

Ernulf School

Ouse Valley Way

Cricket Ground

B1428

Castle Hills

River Mill Boats
All facilities except petrol
☎ 01480 473456

EATON SOCON LOCK
Width 3·3m
Depth 1·6m
Head 2·7m

Sluices Moorings EA
Shallows to about to 0·75m

EATON SOCON

GS Butchers ☎

EA

The Mill Tavern

Weir

Supermarket

Cables
Head 6·1m

Cambridge

A428

Power Station

A1

52 River Great Ouse and tributaries

By a small island, opposite Wray House Farm where in the 1930s there was a ferry, a footpath leads to Great Paxton. Here, surrounded by a beautifully kept grave yard, is a unique Saxon minster church. First built as a cruciform church in the early 11th century, Holy Trinity was rebuilt in the 13th and 15th centuries and restored in 1880. Some Saxon arches remain and as a result of the 13th century rebuilding, the chancel stands some 3m above the nave (key at 7/9 Church Lane). In the village are a few 17th century houses, the Bell public house and a post office and general store.

After Great Paxton, a steep bluff carries the railway line high above the Great Ouse. Another 1·5km upstream, the river turns south west leaving the railway line towards Little Paxton and St Neots Paper Mill Lock. The upstream navigation channel is to the south east of a small island; the downstream channel is to the north west. The Ouse Valley Way, screened from the river by trees and shrubs, passes beside the attractive Paxton Pits Nature Reserve where there is an extensive network of footpaths including a Meadow Trail, Heron trail and circular River Trail. A fenced footpath through private riverside gardens and known as the Hailing Way (a reference to its former use as a tow path) leads the Ouse Valley Way to the Lock

At Little Paxton, whilst many of the old houses were destroyed by a fire in 1945 and there is much modern residential estate development, Paxton Hall, built in c1738 for the son of a Bishop of Lincoln, has traces of earlier work. The stone church of St James, originally a chapel to the minster church at Great Paxton, whilst restored in 1849 and 1896, has a 12th century chancel and an early 15th century square tower.

After St Neots Paper Mills lock, where paper has been manufactured at Samuel Jones factory for over 150 years, the river becomes wide as it turns south past the confluence with the River Kym and Crosshall Marina (diesel and water). Large private lawns sweep down to the river on the west and on the east are Island Common and Lammas Meadow, ancient common lands now managed as Sites of Special Scientific Interest. There is a short length of Huntingdonshire District Council 24 hour moorings just downstream of the private Ouse Valley River Club and Marina.

The Ouse Valley Way crosses the navigation channel at St Neots Paper Mills lock and the main course of the Great Ouse on an elevated walkway, continues on the road briefly, crosses Island Common and rejoins the river bank for a short distance before passing round the Ouse Valley River Club towards St Neots.

The river now flows between Eaton Ford and Eaton Socon to the west and St Neots and Eynesbury to the east. This 'conurbation' lying between the A1 on the west and the railway line on the east developed from early settlements at Eynesbury and Eaton Socon.

Within the parish of Eynesbury a Benedictine Priory of St Neot, a monk of Glastonbury who had educated King Alfred and whose relics had been stolen from Cornwall, was founded in 972. First belonging to Ely, it was destroyed during the Danish wars only to be refounded in the late 11th century when it became subject to the French Abbey of Bec. It was further restored in c1130 by Lady Aroysia de Clare. After some decline in the early 15th century when during the Hundred Years War it was seized as it was considered to be 'foreign', it grew again only to be abandoned after the Dissolution of the Monasteries in the mid 16th century. Possibly its stones were used for the stone bridge built later in that century and whilst the gate-house remained until 1814, there are now no remains, the site having been built over by William Fowler's (later John Day's) brewery in the late 18th and early 19th century.

Today the parish of Eynesbury occupies the area south of St Neots and from which it is separated by the Hen Brook. Effectively a suburb of St Neots with much modern residential and industrial development, the oldest buildings, some half timbered 16th and 17th century houses and the church of St Mary, are gathered in a small conservation area between the Hen Brook and the church. The Brook runs between St Neots Marina and a number of new and restored buildings and old warves of Paines Brewery and between the Woolpack and the Chequers Inn and Restaurant at the road bridge. The church, restored in 1858, has some 12th century remains and a late 17th century tower rebuilt after the earlier tower had collapsed in 1685 destroying much of the chancel and nave. It is said that the 'Eynesbury Giant', 2·6m high when he died aged twenty in 1818, is buried under the font so as to frustrate the attentions of body snatchers. Behind the church, Montague Street leads past Montague House and the Woolpack and Plough Pubs to the river, the

B1428

A428

A1

Wyboston Leisure Park

Golf Course

Restaurant

Power Station

8 overhead power cables in this stretch, min hm 6·1m

10·0m

LITTLE BARFORD
No shops ☎

Railway

N

10·0m

Mile 1

1 Kilometre (Approx)

Shallow

WYBOSTON

Gravel pits

A1

Small holdings

River Great Ouse

B1043

To Bedford 8 miles

A428

A1

Moorings

Kelpie Marine
All facilities – no Petrol
☎ 01234 870249

Tempsford Bridges

Old Road Bridge
3·1m

New Road Bridge
3·7m

10·0m

ROXTON

Footbridge
Head 4·5m

6·1m

48 hi patrous

Anchor Hotel
H

ROXTON LOCK
Width 4·0m
Depth 1·15m
Head 2·75m

Gravel Pit

A1 South

ROXTON LOCK

To Roxton

To Eaton Socon

Weir

Chain

Footpath to Tempsford

Landing stage

To Gt. Barford

Landing stages for use in conjunction with the lock are positioned both above and below Roxton, Great Barford, Willington and Castle Mill locks.

Ouse Valley Way and a riverside caravan park.

Meanwhile, in contrast to the religious developments at Eynesbury, a powerful barony became established around a riverside castle at Eaton Socon (Eaton – village by the water, Socon – special jurisdiction) This Norman castle built on the site of earlier Saxon buildings and consisting of large central mounds with two baileys was strategically positioned to control a River Great Ouse crossing. Although now on private land, it can be clearly seen from the river and the Ouse Valley Way on the east bank.

Also with much recent development, there are a number of inns on the course of the old Great North Road including the Wagon and Horses, the Old Sun and the White Horse and some interesting houses around the Green. The fine parish church was rebuilt to its original form after it had been almost totally destroyed by a fire in 1930. Opposite the south gate in some-what incongruous surroundings is the restored old village lock-up complete with an ancient wooden bed and chains built in 1826 'for the confinement of local malefactors'.

St Neots

The present market town of St Neots gradually became established during the early to mid 12th century between the Priory and the river crossing, where by 1180 a wooden bridge had replaced the ferry. Three fairs were granted during the 13th century and by the 14th century there was a busy river port. St Neots continued to prosper, the wooden bridge being replaced with a stone bridge at the end of the 16th century, which after various modifications was sadly replaced with a modern bridge in 1965. Early businesses, associated with increasing river traffic included lace making, a foundry, paper mills, and malting.

Situated on the route of the old Great North Road, St Neots was to become a well known coaching town as evidenced by the now albeit considerably altered 18th and 19th century houses, shops and coaching inns around the Market Square. Of the several coaching inns only the Old Falcon Hotel and the New Inn remain, the former Cross Keys Hotel now being occupied by a shopping mall leading to car parks and a supermarket. Whilst the Market Square itself has unfortunately lost some of its

former grandeur, restoration is taking place and the early 19th century former Paines Brewery is being renovated by English Heritage. There are all the shops and facilities that one would expect in a market town of this size, with Tourist Information Centres in the public library near the Priory Centre and in the Museum (open Wednesday to Saturday, 1030 to 1630).

The parish church of St Mary, impressive from the outside by its shear size, is not so impressive inside. Whilst a church probably existed here in the 12th century, nothing of that date remains, the earliest being some 13th century and much late 15th century work. There are angels on the roof and animals including lions, griffins, lions, horses, rams and dogs on the cornices. The eastern bay has a painted roof.

Moving upstream, past the Ouse Valley River Club and the St Neots Rowing Club is the Priory Centre and Public Library. Built near the site of the old Priory and incorporating an 18th century oast house, the Centre, with its licensed snack bar, is used for arts, entertainment, leisure and recreation. Public mooring is available along the frontage. Between the Centre and the Town Bridge is the Bridge House Restaurant and Pub with a riverside garden. The Ouse Valley Way wends its way from Lammas Meadow along Priory Path, through a car park, past the Priory Centre, the 18th century Priory House and the site of the Priory gate-house to reach the Town Bridge where it crosses the river to the west bank. The way-marks through St Neots are not very easy to find.

Upstream beyond the bridge the river flows between, on the east, the back of the Old Falcon Hotel, a pleasant new housing development and St Neots Marina at the confluence with the Hen Brook (chandlery, gas, diesel, toilets and moorings, ☎ 01480 472411) and on the west, St Neots Riverside Park (no mooring) to pass under a wooden footbridge. Here the Ouse Valley Way, which had crossed the river on the Town Bridge, re-crosses to the east bank which it then follows to Eaton Socon Lock where it finishes its 42km journey through Huntingdonshire. By the bridge on land subject to a planning proposal is a large old wooden former Broads cruiser, the 'Princess Alexandra'. Continuing past a caravan park, there are views downstream to St Neots church and upstream to Eaton Socon church.

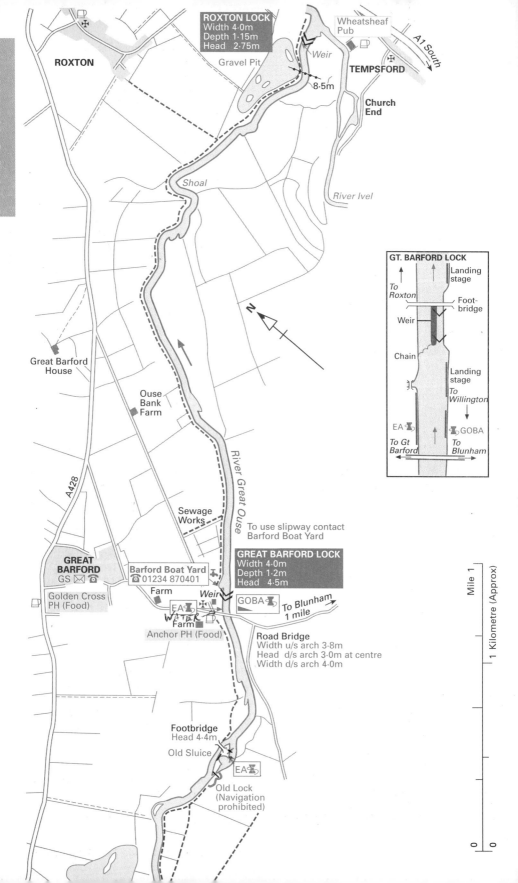

ROXTON LOCK
Width 4·0m
Depth 1·15m
Head 2·75m

ROXTON

Gravel Pit

Wheatsheaf Pub

A1 South

Weir

8·5m

TEMPSFORD

Church End

Shoal

River Ivel

N

Great Barford House

Ouse Bank Farm

River Great Ouse

A428

Sewage Works

To use slipway contact Barford Boat Yard

GREAT BARFORD
GS

Golden Cross PH (Food)

Barford Boat Yard
☎ 01234 870401

Farm

GREAT BARFORD LOCK
Width 4·0m
Depth 1·2m
Head 4·5m

Weir

EA
WATER
Farm

Anchor PH (Food)

GOBA

To Blunham 1 mile

Road Bridge
Width u/s arch 3·8m
Head d/s arch 3·0m at centre
Width d/s arch 4·0m

Footbridge
Head 4·4m

Old Sluice

EA

Old Lock
(Navigation prohibited)

GT. BARFORD LOCK

To Roxton

Landing stage

Foot-bridge

Weir

Chain

Landing stage

To Willington

EA

GOBA

To Gt Barford

To Blunham

Mile 1

1 Kilometre (Approx)

0

0

St Neots to Great Barford

Immediately upstream of the remains of the Norman castle on the west bank is the entrance to River Mill Boats (chandlery, diesel, water, gas, moorings, boat sales and boat hire ☎ 01480 473456); the navigation channel to the lock flows to the east. The converted 19th century mill houses not only the marina, chandlery and offices but The River Mill Tavern (free house, bar meals, restaurant, tea room, gallery) and a ladies health and beauty centre.

For a short distance above the lock the river forms the county boundary between Cambridgeshire and Bedfordshire. Here the view to the east is marred by a new Superstore and massive grey cooling chimneys of Little Barford Power Station. A waymarked and in places overgrown bankside footpath continues on the east side of the river under the busy St Neots bypass, past an industrial area and Little Barford power station, after which it leaves the riverside and crosses a field to the village of Little Barford itself (no facilities).

The redundant church of St Dennis, with some mid 12th century and early-14th-century stonework and a mid 16th-century brass, was once at the centre of a riverside village which, judging by the large area of hummocky ground, must have been quite a size. There was a ferry and the crossing could be hazardous; in December 1297 four people were drowned whilst attempting the passage with a load of flour and a few years later the ferry-man himself was drowned. Possibly due to the building of stone bridges at Great Barford and St Neots, the ferry trade declined and the village migrated east away from the river towards the road. Here in a thatched cottage to the east of the road at the entrance to the small village the 17th/18th century Poet Laureate Nicholas Rowe was born in 1673.

For the next 3km pedestrian access to the river is restricted; there is no footpath on the east bank whilst on the west bank is Wyboston Leisure Park and Golf Course followed by a number of private smallholdings. However immediately after a bank of trees on the east, where the countryside gives way to open fields, there is a footpath which leads to Tempsford where it crosses the river to Roxton and Roxton Lock.

Approaching Tempsford and, on the west bank, Kelpie Marine (moorings, diesel, ☎ 01234 870249), the two carriage-ways of the A1 Trunk Road cross the river on separate bridges, the first modern concrete, the second early 19th century stone. It seems hard to believe now that as late as the 1770s, the only crossing here was by ferry, the first bridge being built in c1800. A century earlier the Great North Road crossed the river at a ford just upstream of the stone bridge. The nearby Tempsford Staunch (built in 1674 and only finally removed in the 1970s) was kept open as long as possible to ensure a shallow crossing. Only when road traffic was light was it closed so that navigation could proceed. Some say that the marshy area around the ford, which readily turned into a swamp in the winter, was John Bunyan's 'Slough of Despond'.

A footbridge links Roxton on the west with Tempsford on the east. Lying off the main road, there is no principal village street in Roxton, although the many of the houses are old. In the parish church of St Mary, mostly 14th century with a low 15th century tower is a mutilated recessed tomb of an unknown 14th century lady in long robes. Behind a large hedge, the Congregational Church is unusual having a thatched roof, tree-trunk veranda and gothic style windows. Food is available at the Royal Oak public house; there are no shops.

Tempsford village on the A1 Trunk Road (considerable traffic noise) is in two parts separated by Tempsford Hall. Built in 1898 in Elizabethan style on the site of an older house, the red brick Hall is the head office of the Kier Group. To the north in Langford End are the riverside gardens of the Anchor Hotel (bar meals and mooring for patrons).

The southern part of the village with its restored 14th and 15th century church of St Peter lies on the old Great North Road sandwiched between the A1 and the River Ivel which joins the River Great Ouse just below Roxton Lock. Gannock's Castle is an ancient, overgrown moated site almost certainly all that remains of the fortress built by the Danes in 921 when they were advancing from Huntingdon to Bedford. They had thought that by operating from Tempsford they would command a wider field, however after their defeat at Bedford they returned to the fortress only to be attacked by King Edward the Elder in the summer of the same year. The fortress was taken and the Danish king and his sons killed. (Gannock –

10·0m

Mill
Farm
Footbridge

Weir

WILLINGTON LOCK
Width 4·0m
Depth 1·3m
Head 4·05m

Gadsey Brook

A428

Sewage
Works

WILLINGTON

Danish Camp
Day boat hire, Coffee shop

Water
End

10·0m

Great
Dairy
Farm

✠
NOTE
There are no moorings
between the old lock
above Great Barford
and the Sewage Works
Bridge, Goldington

10·0m

Howbury
Hall

Bedford to Sandy Country Way

Road Bridge
6·2m

A421

CASTLE MILL LOCK
Width 4·0m
Depth 1·2m
Head 4·3m
Fall 2·7m

Weir

Castle
Dairy
Farm

Bedford
Castle Mill
Airfield

Risinghoe
Castle
(Motte)

Weir

N

River Great Ouse

A428

GOLDINGTON

Sewage Works
Bridge
2·6m

GOBA

*Navigation
Channel*

New cut

WILLINGTON LOCK

Landing
stage

To Gt. Barford

To Willington

Weir

Chain

To
Castle Mill

Landing
stage

CASTLE MILL LOCK

To Willington

Landing
stage

Bridleway
To A428

Bridleway

Chain

Bedford
Castle Mill
Airfield

To Bedford

CARDINGTON LOCK

Weir

To Cardington

Landing
stage

Landing
stage

*To
Bedford*

*To Priory
Country Park*

**CARDINGTON
LOCK**
Width 3·15m
Depth 1·15m
Head 2·75m

Priory
Business
Park

*Sluice
Gate*

Weir

a corruption of Dannicke, Danes work or village fortification?)

In the village are the 15th century timber framed Gannock House, Tingey's House (1534), the Wheatsheaf Inn, formerly the George (bar meals). There are no shops.

The River Ivel flowing from Hitchin and once navigable for lighters as far Biggleswade joins the River Great Ouse at Tempsford. There is a theory that the timber used for the construction of the Octagon Tower in Ely Cathedral in 1341 was transported from forests at Chicksands down the Ivel and then down the Great Ouse to Ely. If this is the case then it either pre-supposes that the stretch of river between Earith and Ely was complete by the 14th century, supporting the theory that many of the early changes to the natural river courses were made during the period of monastic building or that the Roman Car Dyke was still a major route. (See The Old West River, Pope's Corner to Stretham.)

Continuing upstream from the junction with the River Ivel and Roxton Lock, the River Great Ouse flows west passing fir trees screening an attractive privately managed lake, to reach after about 1·5km a sharp bend of nearly 360° with shoals on the inside. This bend precedes a series of bends interspersed with straight stretches before a final straight leads under a footbridge to Great Barford lock. Between the two locks the river flows between quite steep banks (no mooring) with flat open country-side to the south and east and rising ground to the north and west. There is a well way-marked public bridleway between Roxton and Great Barford on the north and west bank. Whilst described as a bridleway, it is little more than a narrow and at times very overgrown foot-path. Shortly after passing through a private garden it leaves the riverside, goes round a sewage works and then follows the road back to the river at Great Barford bridge just upstream from Great Barford Lock.

From the river, the most striking aspect of Great Barford is the part 15th century stone bridge with its 17 irregular arches and upstream cutwaters. Sir Gerard Braybroke, in his will of 1429, wished that a bridge 'be performed and finished' and in 1441 the Burgers of Bedford appealed for rent for a bridge to be built. It was substantially repaired in 1777 and widened somewhat unattractively on the upstream side in brick. For many years up to the Civil War, Great Barford was at the head of navigation and there were many wharves and pubs. However some 15 years after the building of great Barford Staunch in 1674 navigation went right up to Bedford.

Behind the popular Anchor Inn (formerly the Bull) is the parish church of All Saints. It has been largely rebuilt in 14th century style, the only old parts being the 15th century tower and some possibly Anglo-Danish work in the chancel where there are a late 16th century marble and alabaster monument and two early 16th century brasses.

The village extends past some large houses up to a post office and stores and the busy Bedford Road on which are the Golden Cross and Beehive Inns.

Great Barford to Bedford

Between Great Barford and Willington Lock, the Ouse flows in a generally south easterly direction initially through open fields which give way to pleasant willow tree lined stretches. After a wood on the south bank, it flows past one a the series of locks first built in the 17th century now made redundant by river improvement schemes. Mooring is possible immediately downstream of the lock in the old navigation channel. (Note: the present navigation channel keeps to the north bank.) The river becomes progressively narrower flowing between quite steep banks. There is an easy waymarked riverside footpath leading from Great Barford, first on the north bank, then crossing the river on a series of wooden footbridges at the site of the old lock to the south bank, to Willington Lock.

From the lock a footpath leads to Willington. The former Bedford to Cambridge railway line (now a footpath and cycle-way linking Great Barford with Priory Marina, Bedford) ran close to the river here and passed through earthworks, ramparts and moats, most likely old Danish docks. Now on private land, surrounded by a high security fence, there would have been space for up to 30 ships accommodating about 2500 men and probably associated with the Danish advance from Huntingdon to Bedford. After the Danes' defeat the 'Docks' became an 11th century moated farmhouse.

In the early 16th century, the major land-owner was Sir John Gostwick who served Cardinal Wolsey and assisted Henry VIII in

the destruction of the Bedfordshire monasteries. Whilst most of his Tudor mansion was burnt down, a fine early 16th century stone dovecote with stepped gables, a two tiered roof and holes for 1400 pigeons and a stone stable also with stepped gables, two floors, good roof and fireplace remain near the church of St Laurence. The stone for these buildings, now in the care of the National Trust (open April to end September by appointment ☎ 01234 838278) probably came from Newnham Priory in Bedford after its destruction. The buff stone church is historically important as it is all of late perpendicular style probably built by Sir John and to whose family there are alabaster monuments.

In the village are a few thatched cottages, modern houses, the Crown public house and on the Bedford road, a post office and stores.

Above Willington Lock, the Great Ouse continues east for about 1km with Willington to the south and open fields to the north, before turning sharply to the north west; open fields continue on the east whilst the west bank becomes wooded. After a further 1km the river turns back to the east near a high tree covered bluff at the top of which are some more earthworks again possibly associated with the Danes, then flows under the new Bedford bypass to Castle Mill Lock and, on private land, Risinghoe Castle which, with an apparent motte and bailey may indeed have been a castle, but actually looks more like a barrow, possibly of Viking origin. At Willington Lock a footpath is signed on the north bank. The first short length along the riverside is almost totally overgrown and a path has grown up around this stretch along a field edge. After 0·5km the path leaves the riverside and passes within sight of the river across fields and along farm roads to the A428 Bedford road near the earthworks. Thereafter there is no riverside path until after another 0·5km a path from the A428 (access not ideal but best from opposite the MFI Warehouse) to Castle Mill Lock joins the riverside for a short distance on its south bank, where there is a single grass runway of Bedford (Castle Mill) 'Airfield'. There is no footpath between Castle Mill Lock and Cardington Lock however the footpath and cycle-way from Willington to Priory Marina passes relatively close to the river which it crosses just upstream of Bedford sewage works and Cardington Lock.

Although not on the river, the two vast hangers built by the Short Brothers in 1917 and 1927 to house the R100 and R101 airships which had been made there, lie to the south at Cardington. The R101 was to crash in flames at Beauvais in France on 5 October 1930 during her maiden voyage to India with the loss of 49 lives. They are remembered in St Mary's parish church where the airship's scorched ensign hangs above a memorial plaque; their tomb is in the churchyard to the north west of the church across the street.

St Mary's was almost entirely rebuilt, on the site of an earlier Norman church, during 1898/1901 largely by the Whitbread family. In the nave are two fine 16th and 17th century monuments with excellent brasses. The Whitbread Chapel is a memorial to the Whitbread family including Samuel Whitbread who, in the mid 18th century founded the well known Whitbread Brewery. He, together with John Howard who did much to reform prisons throughout Europe, bought and improved much of Cardington; the 18th century houses around the church and Green, where the King's Arms public house serves meals, along with other old houses bearing the initials SW are a testament to their efforts. A little to the west, in about 1917, the Short Brothers built the garden village of Shortstown for their labourers.

At Cardington Lock footpaths lead to Priory Country Park (nature reserves, nature trails, lakes, sailing, picnic areas, etc), Cardington Village and along the north river bank to Bedford and beyond to Kempston Mill. The river flows past the Barns Hotel, a former 17th century manor house with a medieval tithe barn (mooring for patrons), a weir on the north bank feeding the Cardington Canoe Slalom, Bedford Boat Club moorings and round a bend towards Priory Marina, the entrance to which is crossed by a high footbridge. Amongst the facilities at the marina are fuel, a chandlery, moorings, workshops and day boat hire ☎ 01234 351931. Adjoining the marina is Priory Marina Beefeater Restaurant and close by is Aspects Leisure Centre with a Megabowl bowling alley, night-club, 6 screen cinema and restaurants. The modern triangular building on the opposite bank is the Oasis Beach swimming pool.

Nearby is the site of the Augustinian Newnham Priory, of which only a few overgrown earthworks, considerably altered

Weir

Priory Country Party

Barns Hotel

Canoe Slalom Course

Weir

Industial Estate

Priory Marina
(All facilities)
☎ (01234) 351931

Bedford Boat Club

Bedford to Sandy Country Way
New Cut

A5140

A428

GOBA

Railway Bridge 2·3m

Footbridge 2·9m

Road Bridge 2·7m

A603 FENLAKE

Russell Park

Superstore, filling station and Aqua Sports Centre accessible via footpath

Mill Meadows

Footbridge 2·1m

BEDFORD

BEDFORD LOCK
Width 3·3m
Depth 1·1m
Head 2·05m

NEW FENLAKE

A600

Museum

Rowing Club
Moat House Hotel

Road Bridge 3·3m

A6

A6

HM Prison

County Hall

A6

Road Bridge 3·0m

A5141

A5141

A6

EA 48hr Sovereign Quay

Rail Bridge 2·0m

Caution. Do not navigate upstream from moorings - shoaling

Low Cables Approx. 2·9m

Station

Rail Bridge 2·0m

Footbridge 2·7m

B531

A428

Queen's Park

Kempston Grange

KEMPSTON

Mile 1
1 Kilometre (Approx)
0   0

N

BEDFORD LOCK

To A5140

Upper River

Mill Meadow

Lower River

To Cardington

Engineers Bridge

To A6

To Kempston

Weir

John Bunyan Plaque

Abbey Bridge

by the former Cambridge to Bedford railway line, remain. It was one of the oldest foundations in the County, having been built after the succession of Henry II in c1166. Whilst it had a good reputation it suffered when during King John's reign much was pulled down in order to strengthen Bedford Castle. After the castle was captured by King Henry III in c1223 the stone was returned only to be removed again to build Sir John Gostwick's house in Willington, after the Priory was surrendered in 1540/41.

Between the A5140 road bridge and the Town Bridge, Mill Meadows form an island between two branches of the River Great Ouse known as the Upper River, used for rowing and the Lower River, which for most of its way forms the navigation channel and along which it is possible to moor. There is a pleasure boating lake on part of the island; the remainder is maintained, as is the south bank, as a pleasant formal park and garden. Both the south bank of the Lower River and the north bank of the Upper River are tree lined. The first footbridge to cross the Lower River is the Royal Engineers Bridge built for the town in 1934. Further footbridges lead the footpath across Bedford Lock, over Duckmill Weir and Abbey Bridges, to the town bridge and beyond to the County Bridge. Just below the weir on the bank of a small backwater a little round plaque commemorates the baptism of John Bunyan, 'circa 1650'.

The navigation channel locks up into the Upper River. On the north bank is the site of the former Bedford Castle, now incorporated in the Bedford Museum and Gardens and the Cecil Higgins Art Gallery. To the south is the King's Ditch, now just a small watercourse but originally part of King Edward the Elder's defences against the Danish invasion. The river then flows past Bedford Rowing Club, between The Bedford Moat House and The Bedford Swan Hotels, the latter having been previously been built for the Duke of Bedford in 1794 on the site of an earlier house, under the Town Bridge. In the red brick former Shire Hall on the north bank, James Hanratty was found guilty of the 'A6 Murders'. Executed in Bedford prison in 1962, he was the last man to be hanged in Britain. The Great Ouse then flows past Bedford College, the Star Rowing Club, County Hall and under County roadbridge (where the riverside footpath crosses to the

north bank) and two sets of railway bridges into the suburbs of Bedford towards Kempston Mill, the limit of navigation. There are three circular riverside walks between Bedford and Kempston.

Bedford

. . .my great-grandfather was but a waterman, looking one way and rowing another; and I got most of my estate by the same occupation.
John Bunyan

Bedford today is a busy modern county town which probably started as a small settlement, the home of a Saxon chief Beda, which had become established at an important ford across the Great Ouse, Batts Ford. Danelaw spread over the region and a 'Jarl' or Earl was installed at Bedford. Following the Dane's defeat by Edward the Elder in c920, the Earl's 'burgh' was to become Bedfordshire. After the Norman Conquest, a castle was built and it remained until 1223 when it was finally captured and destroyed by King Henry III. The town prospered, religious houses at Cauldwell and Newnham were founded, schools were established and a maze of streets, where in 1439 there was a stampede in which 18 people were suffocated or trampled to death, grew up around a small guildhall. The area around St Paul's Square and the nearby car park was only cleared in about 1800.

Bedford should be justly proud of its sons, adopted or otherwise, and which include Glenn Miller, John Howard, Sir William Harpur and John Bunyan.

An adopted son was the band leader Glenn Miller who, with his band, was based in Bedford during the Second World War. It was from there that he not only made many of his broadcasts but he also flew to entertain the Allied troops on mainland Europe.

In the second half of the 18th century, John Howard forcefully put forward the case for prison reform. In 1777 he presented his survey 'The State of Prisons' following his visits to prisons both in Britain and on the Continent. He demanded that prisons and the infamous prison ships be improved and although early progress was slow, it was the start of a world wide movement of reform. His legacy is the Howard League of Penal Reform.

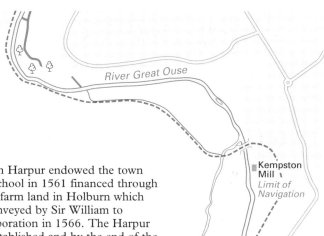

Sir William Harpur endowed the town with a free school in 1561 financed through some 7ha of farm land in Holburn which had been conveyed by Sir William to Bedford corporation in 1566. The Harpur Trust was established and by the end of the 19th century it had provided schools through-out Bedford, four of which namely Bedford School, Bedford High School, Bedford Modern School and Dame Alice School remain today as trust schools.

Arguably however the most famous son of Bedford was John Bunyan. Born a few miles away from Bedford at Elstow in 1628, he was drafted into the Parliamentary Army at the outbreak of the Civil War aged just 16. At 19 he was discharged and shortly after married his first wife by whom he was to have four children, one of them being a blind girl and of whom he was particularly fond. Despite a love of dancing, bell ringing and an almost irresistible desire to swear during holy occasions, he had from his youth been haunted by religious fears and he was oppressed by a sense of sin. He found a degree of peace through joining a strict Non-conformist congregation in Bedford and he became close to their pastor John Gifford. In 1655, when his first wife died, he moved into Bedford and his gift for preaching became recognised. However after the Restoration of the Monarchy in 1660, non-conformists such as John Bunyan were forbidden to preach. He refused and was sentenced to stay in prison until he conformed. He was 32 when he was taken to the County Jail where he was to remain despite appeals by his second wife Elizabeth, until his release 12 years later under a General Pardon in 1672.

He rapidly became famous both as a preacher and a writer but some 3 years later he was arrested and imprisoned again but this time only for six months. It was during this period that he wrote the first part of The Pilgrim's Progress, the complete work being published in February 1678. During his life-time 100,00 copies were sold and it was to become one of the best known books in the world and to be translated into more than 150 languages and dialects. John Bunyan died of pneumonia in 1688 and is buried in London.

There remains much related to John Bunyan in Bedford and the Tourist Information Office in St Paul's Square ☎ 01234 215226 describes the places of interest in a useful and informative guide.

Bedford to Kempston Mill

After the two sets of railway bridges, the Great Ouse flows between private moorings on the south and, screened by trees, Charles Wells' Eagle Brewery on the north bank, into park land with weeping willow trees. A riverside footpath crosses on the Queens Bridge shortly after which the navigation channel keeps to the south of some small islands near a housing estate (where the footpath can easily be accessed). With open fields to the north and houses to the south, the river flows to the ancient site of Kempston Mill, destroyed by fire in 1969. In 1892, a Bill was drawn up to extend the navigation via 30km of canals and 25 locks to the Grand Junction Canal. However vigorous opposition to the Bill from the railway companies, Bedford Corporation and Bedfordshire County Council caused the Bill to be dropped and Kempston remains the effective limit of navigation.

The River Wissey, Little Ouse and River Lark

The River Wissey

Confluence with the River Great Ouse to Hilgay

The river is generally one of the more attractive of the Great Ouse's tributaries. It rises near East Braddenham and flows for some 50km to join the Great Ouse. Its original course, however, was not to King's Lynn but to Wisbech, to whom it gave its name. Although its mouth is narrow, it is wide and deep enough for navigation. However navigators should beware of submerged piles, especially where the banks have recently been refurbished between the Great Ouse and Hilgay.

Between the Great Ouse and Hilgay the river meanders between flood banks across low-lying fenland. Throughout this length there is a good footpath on the north bank; the path on the south bank leaves the river just before Hilgay. Upstream of the railway bridge, the land to the north gradually becomes more wooded whilst the land to the south remains low-lying fenland.

The first road bridge, about 3½km from the Great Ouse, just upstream of some private moorings is the A10 Hilgay bypass, almost immediately after which is Hilgay Old Bridge. The riverside village of Hilgay is quite ancient: there are Anglo-Saxon and pre-Domesday references to an abundance of fish and eels; it had ties with Ramsey Abbey; and there are remains of manorial earthworks. It lies on the northwest segment of an almost circular fenland isle which now rises some 20m above the surrounding fen which has been shrinking since drainage commenced. During a 45-year period in the late 19th and early 20th century, the rate of shrinkage locally had been up to 5cm per year.

Whilst Denver was the birthplace of George William Manby, he lived for much of his life in Hilgay at the Elizabethan Wood Hall, once a grange of the Abbots of Ramsey. He was at school with Nelson and was brought up with a military and naval background. After hopelessly witnessing ships in distress, it was at Hilgay that he invented a rocket-like apparatus to throw a line to a ship and it is said that he experimented from the roof of the church tower, where he was church warden! By 1823 use of this mortar had resulted in some 230 lives being saved. For this he was awarded £2,000 by parliament. He died in Yarmouth but is buried in Hilgay where his memorial tablet commemorates his invention.

All Saint's Church is at the end of a beautiful avenue of 60 lime trees interspersed with holly bushes and with a lych-gate at each end. Although there are some 14th century remains, principally the nave with its leaning arcade of two tall and two low arches, severe restoration took place in 1869–70. The brick tower dates from 1794. Inside is an ornate marble pulpit and the wooden lectern originally came from St Peter's Church in Manchester.

In the village there are a post office and off-licence, general stores, garage, the Rose and Crown Inn and, by the old bridge, the Cross Keys Riverside Hotel and Restaurant on one side and a public slipway and Environment Agency moorings on the other.

To the north, across the river and the cut-off channel which, lined with poplars, has a somewhat continental character, is the hamlet of Fordham, with its small flint and carstone chapel and three fine Georgian houses.

Hilgay to Wissington

After leaving Hilgay and passing between the Environment Agency moorings and a second length of Denver Cruising Club moorings, the river meanders pleasantly for the next 2½km along the open edge of Hilgay Fen. Throughout this length, and indeed all the way to Wissington, there is a path and flood bank to the north. In places this path is very overgrown – particularly near Jubilee Wood. Whilst it is just passable

River Great Ouse
See page 14

See page 14

Railway Ely-King's Lynn

SILT FEN

*To Denver
1 mile*

Ouse Bridge
4.0m

Wissey Bridge
2.7m

GOBA

River Great Ouse

Ten Mile Bank

River Wissey

*To Littleport
8 miles*

GREAT WEST
FEN

Gravelhouse
Farm

FORDHAM
FEN

N

FORDHAM

A10

Mile 1

1 Kilometre (Approx)

Cross Keys
Hotel

Bridges
2.6m

6.1m

A10

*To Downham
Market (2 mile*

Slipway

*To Southery
3 miles*

Rose &
Crown
☎ 01366
385414

WC
EA

6.1m

Snowre
Hall

HILGAY
GS ✉ But ☎

*Watch for
concrete
under
water*

Skipwith
Corner

Cut-off Channel

0

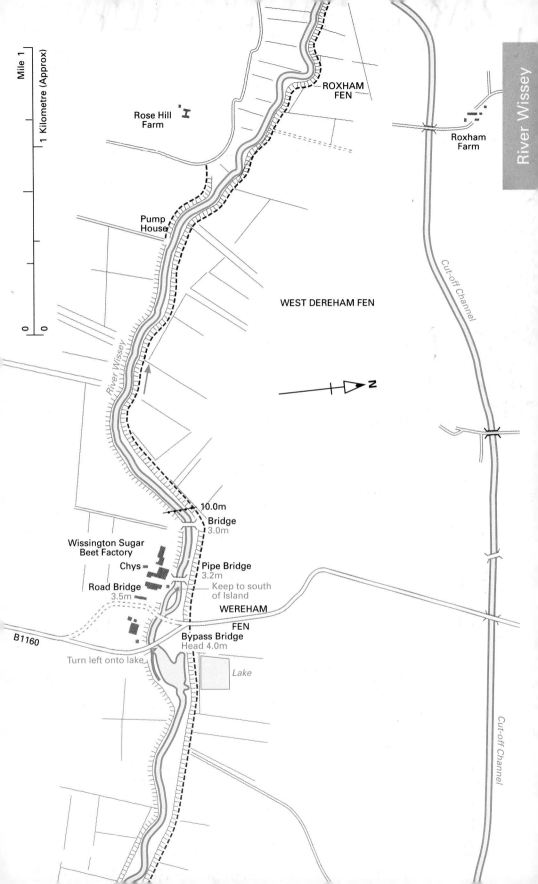

Mile 1

1 Kilometre (Approx)

0

Rose Hill Farm

ROXHAM FEN

Roxham Farm

Pump House

Cut-off Channel

WEST DEREHAM FEN

N

River Wissey

10.0m

Bridge 3.0m

Wissington Sugar Beet Factory

Chys

Pipe Bridge 3.2m

Road Bridge 3.5m

Keep to south of Island

WEREHAM

FEN

Bypass Bridge
Head 4.0m

B1160

Turn left onto lake

Lake

Cut-off Channel

during the winter, it becomes virtually impassable during the summer.

Near Skipwith Corner, where the river is close to the poplar-lined cut-off channel, Snowre or Snore Hall which dates from the mid-15th century can be glimpsed through the trees to the north. Originally it was a simple oblong building with buttresses at each corner and walls of exceptional thickness. The 15th-century brickwork on the west side is one of the earliest examples of domestic brickwork in the England. There are Elizabethan and Jacobean windows on the south and the front was much restored in the 19th century. Inside is a secret chamber measuring some 6m by 3m and where, in April 1646, Charles I is said to have hidden on his way from Oxford to King's Lynn where he was hoping either to gain support or to escape. He was unsuccessful in both and eventually gave himself up in Newark.

After Jubilee Wood, the river runs between flood banks towards the riverside Wissington Sugar Factory which, for miles around, dominates the landscape not only by its sheer size, but during the autumn by countless lorry and tractor loads of sugar-beet clogging the local roads, plumes of steam reaching high into the sky and the all-pervading smell of the sugar production process.

At first it might seem strange that such a large factory should ever have been built in a relatively remote part of fenland. Indeed when it was built in 1925 there was not even road access. It was, however, in the centre of the sugar-beet growing area and was served by both the river and the Wissington Light Railway.

This standard-gauge light railway, built in 1905 without either an Act of Parliament or a Light Railway Order, was opened in 1906 for the benefit of local farms. It ran from Abbey Junction, near Station Farm on the north bank of the modern cut-off channel, on the Denver to Stoke Ferry Railway, for about 16km across the river and privately owned fenland to its terminus at Poppylot between Southery and Feltwell.

In 1925 the predecessors of British Sugar leased the line and extended it a further 13km into the surrounding fenland to ensure adequate supplies of sugar-beet. During the war, because of its strategic importance to the country, it was taken over by the Ministry of Agriculture in March 1941 and reconditioned by Italian prisoners of war, who also built the first roads to the factory. Although there were no telephones or signals and there were right-angle bends in the track, trains of a hundred trucks of agricultural produce regularly left the Abbey sidings.

The Ministry purchased the railway in 1947 and ran it in its entirety until 1957 when all lines beyond the factory were closed. The line was finally closed in April 1965. One of the last three steam engines, a Hudswell Clark 0-6-0ST locomotive, *Wissington*, is now preserved on the North Norfolk Railway at Sheringham.

Wissington to Whittington

At Wissington (car parking difficult) there is a dramatic improvement in the north bank footpath which is maintained to Whittington. Once past the sugar factory the river is very attractive, flowing first through two 'lakes' and then meandering in washlands between well set-back flood banks. After the junction with Methwold Lode there is no flood bank on the south and that on the north becomes less significant. The river then crosses the cut-off channel in a concrete aqueduct, flows under the control sluice (headroom limited to 2·9m by an upstream concrete footbridge) to reach Stoke Ferry.

Referred to as 'Stoches' in the Domesday Book (stow = a dwelling; ches = by the water), a fair and market were granted by Henry III in 1239. An interest was given to the English Gilbertine Canon's House of Shouldham. It is said that, because the Canon imposed such high tolls on the ferry at Stoke Ferry, the villagers built a bridge. The Canon duly destroyed it, but he was summoned, found guilty of the bridge's destruction and ordered to rebuild it. The early market fell into disuse and, in 1426, a second charter was granted by Henry VI for a market and fair to be held on 6 December. This has never been revoked and indeed the market continued until the end of the 19th century.

During the 18th and 19th centuries, Stoke Ferry prospered as an inland port and major trading centre. It was described at the time as a handsome, pleasant town on the bank of the Stoke River. Although now perhaps in need of some revitalisation, there are a number of pleasing houses including: All Saints Lodge with its Dutch gables, previously the Crown Hotel, parts of which may date from the 13th century; the

River Wissey

Stoke Ferry Farm

Catsholm House

STOKE FERRY FEN

Methwold Lode

River Wissey

Cut-off Channel

Herringay Hill

Limehouse Farm

Aqueduct

NORTHWOLD FEN

Sluice open at times of flood

Sluices

Pumping Station

Sluice closed at times of flood

Bluebell PH
☎ 01366 500358

Millers Arms PH
☎ 01366 500275

Road Bridge
2.5m

Stoke Ferry Bridge
2.5m

STOKE FERRY
E.cl - Tuesday
GS ✉ ☎

Mile 1

1 Kilometre (Approx)

A134

Roadbridge
2.9m

GOBA
Showers GS Garage

B1112

A134

WHITTINGTON

Stringside Drain

Head of Navigation

Long Craft may turn at junction with Stringside Drain (unnavigable). Long craft may turn at junction

Crown, formerly the King's Arms dating from 1670; the Elizabethan Canterbury House; two 17th century merchant's houses – the Cobbles and Bayfields; and the imposing red-brick late 18th century Hall. In the centre is Favor Parker's mill.

The redundant parish church of All Saints, on the site of a much earlier church, was largely rebuilt in the 1760s following the collapse of the tower in 1758 and there was further rebuilding in 1848.

In the village there is a licensed general stores, post office, fish and chip shop and an engineering and hardware store. At the rear of the Favor Parker Canteen (open to the public Monday to Friday until 2.30pm) is the Miller's Arms public house (bar meals). On the riverside, new houses stand where there used to be staithes, and the former Bull Public House, built in 1930 after a fire had destroyed the old Bull Inn and where an inn had existed for centuries, is being converted into flats.

At Whittington a little upstream and to the east of Stoke Ferry, wharves and kilns were used in the 19th century by Whitbread's brewery and until the end of that century there was nearby a working 'whiting peg mill'. This consisted of a circular trough filled with chalk and water which were then crushed and mixed by a heavy roller pulled round by a pony. The slurry was allowed to set, cut into briquettes and sold as a whitewash.

Whittington, with its stretch of GOBA moorings, caravan park and facilities immediately upstream of the busy A134 road bridge on the south bank, is presently at the limit of navigation and at the end of the riverside path. All craft can turn at the junction with the Stringside Drain.

The Little Ouse River or Brandon Creek

Two springs, separated by only a few metres, rise between Redgrave in Suffolk and South Lopham in Norfolk. One flows west and is the source of the River Waveney; the other flows east and is the source of the River Little Ouse. For much of their length the two rivers form the boundary between Norfolk and Suffolk and indeed but for the few metres separating the springs, Norfolk would be an island. The Little Ouse is joined by two tributaries, the Sapiston and Thet, before it flows through Thetford and crosses first Breckland and then remote and lonely fenland to join the Great Ouse at Brandon Creek.

Now covered with vast plantations of pine, larch and spruce, Breckland is a primeval region where among sandy and flinty heaths, warrens and woodlands, primitive Mesolithic and Neolithic man once lived and worked, mining the black flint which he 'knapped' (split and shaped) to make his tools and weapons. Over 300 mines have been traced, one of which, Grimes Graves north of Weeting, is open to the public (English Heritage, ☎ 01473 265675 for opening times). Here, 10m below ground, galleries radiate from a central shaft like spokes in a wheel. There are remains of picks made from the antlers of red deer and some of the earliest drawings ever found in Britain. Knapping has continued here for thousands of years and not only for peaceful purposes; millions of flints were produced for Wellington's Peninsular War and indeed they were supplied until relatively recently to equip the old flintlocks used by African tribesmen.

There were two other important trades in Breckland: brick-making and, until the spread of myxomatosis, a large-scale trade in rabbit fur, from the thousands of rabbits which lived in the sandy heaths and warrens, for clothes and hats.

Until the middle of the 18th century, Breckland was a dry, treeless, uncultivated and steppe-like region where there were sandstorms. One particular storm, the Great Sand Flood of 1668, blew sand from Lakenheath Warren for about 8km, almost covering Santon Downham and completely damming the Little Ouse.

The river has a long history of navigation. There are 13th century references to water-borne services to Brandon and Hockwold and, before Denver Sluice was built, large barges went up to Thetford. However, once the sluice had been built, stopping the tide, river levels fell. In 1670 an Act for the improvement of navigation on the Little Ouse was introduced. Staunches were built but, because they were far apart, there were long delays whilst the water levels built up sufficiently to enable navigation to continue. A hundred years later, an ambitious proposal was made to link the Little Ouse at Thetford with the River Stort at Bishops Stortford by a canal. A connecting spur to Cambridge would have meant that goods from King's Lynn and all over East Anglia could have reached London by water at a quarter of the cost of road transport. However the quantities were insufficient to justify the capital cost and the scheme was finally abandoned in the mid-1850s with the advent of the railways. Today the river is navigable to Brandon.

There are footpaths on the north and south banks between Brandon Creek and Botany Bay where there is a short gap. While the path on the north bank then continues to Brandon, the path on the south side is not always by the river, neither is it continuous.

Brandon Creek to Hockwold cum Wilton

For about 10km between Brandon Creek and Botany Bay, the River Little Ouse runs in a straight southeast/northwest man-made channel, probably of Roman origin. Its early natural course from Botany Bay was due west to Littleport where it joined the River Great Ouse near Old Bank Farm. This course can still easily be traced along some of the best examples of rodhams in East Anglia. These cross and recross the A1101 showing up as light-coloured silt bands standing proud of dark, low-lying fenland soils.

Moving upstream from the Ship Inn at Brandon Creek, under the busy A10 trunk road and past a stretch of private moorings, the river, bordered by rows of poplars to the south, flows past Burnt Fen, which, according to legend had been set alight by Hereward the Wake. On the north bank, a by-road gives way after about 1km to a good bridleway which goes on alongside the river through the middle of a small gravel island on which are built the hamlets, linked by a cock-up bridge, of Little Ouse with its small flint and brick former Church of St

John (1869) and Brandon Creek.

The river continues through a very remote part of fenland, passing under a farm bridge at Redmere Fen, site of the former 15th century Redmoor House, to cross its early course near Old Decoy Farm. Decoys, devices into which wild birds were lured, sometimes by tame ducks, only to be caught by waiting wildfowlers, were a common 18th century feature of the fenland landscape.

Two barely discernible tributaries join the Little Ouse at the marshy Botany Bay; first is Lakenheath Old Lode or Cross Water and, second, Lakenheath New Lode or Stallode. A few metres upstream near the remains of a staunch, the river returns to its natural course at a spot sometimes called Green Dragon Corner after a former Inn that had existed on the south bank.

The relatively wide river, with a good footpath on the north bank, then meanders within flood banks past washes, meres and intermittent wooded stretches across lonely open fenland towards Wilton road bridge. The road leads south to the nearby Lakenheath railway station and, after 5km, to Lakenheath itself with its vast and sometimes noisy airfield, presently a home of the USAF. To the north across the cut-off channel is Hockwold cum Wilton.

Hockwold cum Wilton to Brandon

Near the red-brick Tudor Hockwold Hall is the now-redundant Hockwold Parish Church of St Peter. Dating largely from the 14th century, but with some possible Saxon remains, it has early wall paintings and a fine low-pitched roof where curved tie beams alternate with hammer beams and eight saints, some crowned, look down with upraised hands. (The key is kept at the Old Bull House.)

Wilton adjoins Hockwold and on a small green is an ancient, slender, stone pillar put up to commemorate Queen Victoria's Diamond Jubilee in 1897. The early 14th century Parish Church of St James has on its tower a recessed stone spire – a rare sight in Norfolk. Behind the church are the remains of six fish ponds referred to in the Domesday Book.

There are two pubs: the thatched New Inn at Hockwold (bed and breakfast and bar food); and the Red Lion facing the small green in Wilton (bar food).

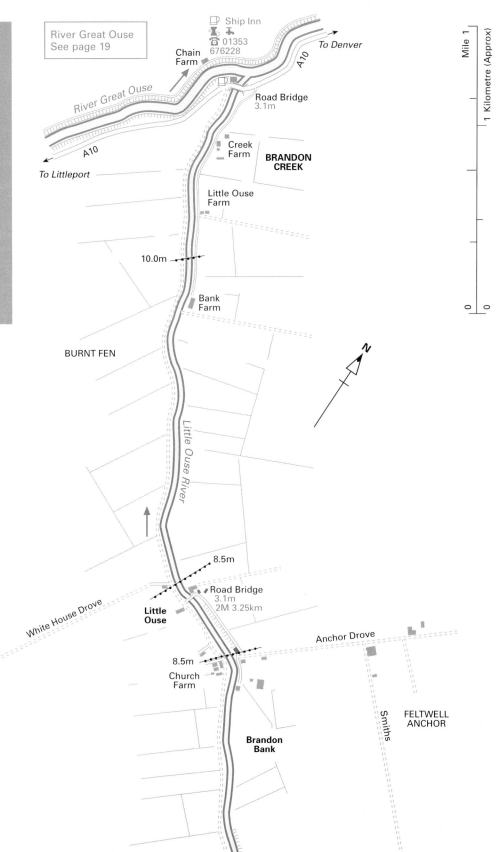

River Wissey, Little Ouse and Lark

River Great Ouse
See page 19

Ship Inn
☎ 01353
676228

To Denver

Chain
Farm

River Great Ouse

Road Bridge
3.1m

A10

To Littleport

A10

Creek
Farm

BRANDON
CREEK

Little Ouse
Farm

10.0m

Bank
Farm

BURNT FEN

N

Little Ouse River

8.5m

White House Drove

Road Bridge
3.1m
2M 3.25km

Little
Ouse

Anchor Drove

8.5m

Church
Farm

Smiths

FELTWELL
ANCHOR

Brandon
Bank

Mile 1

1 Kilometre (Approx)

0

0

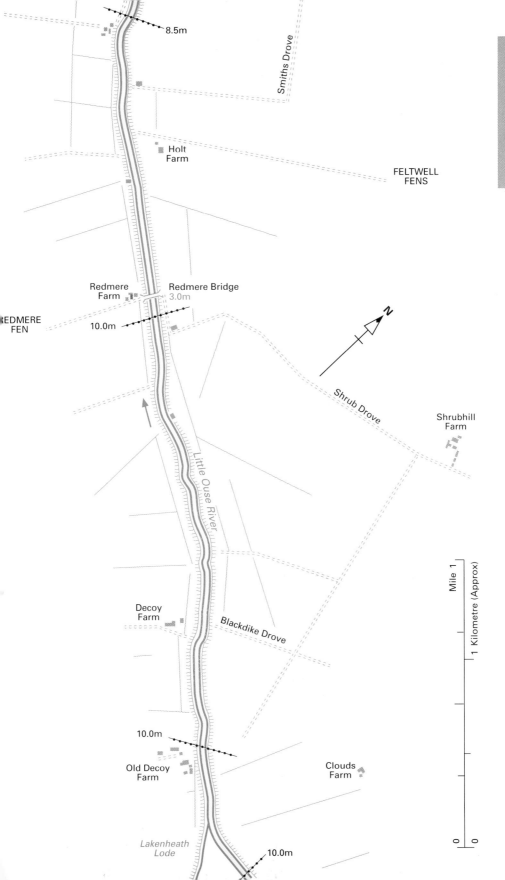

8.5m

Smiths Drove

Holt
Farm

FELTWELL
FENS

Redmere
Farm

Redmere Bridge
3.0m

REDMERE
FEN

10.0m

N

Shrub Drove

Shrubhill
Farm

Little Ouse River

Decoy
Farm

Blackdike Drove

Mile 1

1 Kilometre (Approx)

10.0m

Old Decoy
Farm

Clouds
Farm

Lakenheath
Lode

10.0m

0

Lakenheath
Lode

Botany
Bay

10.0m

Cross Water Staunch
Keep to left channel

Site of old
Stop Lock

Pumping
Station

GOBA

N

NORFOLK

Norfolk
Farm

FEN

Headland Drove

SHEPHERD
FEN

Meres

Meres

JOIST FEN

HOCKWOLD
FEN

Tree
Plantations

Little Ouse River

Railway

NEW
FEN

Cowlie's Drove

Tree
Plantations

BRANDON
FEN

Mile 1

1 Kilometre (Approx)

0

0

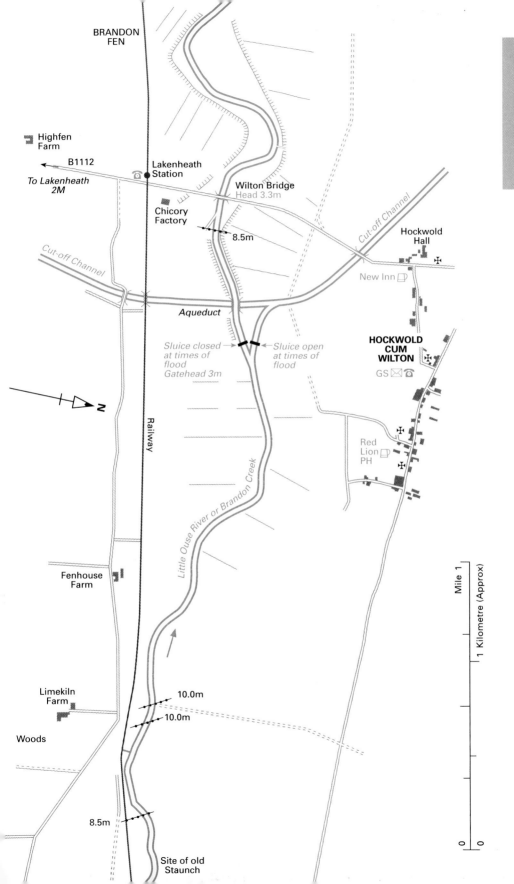

BRANDON FEN

Highfen Farm

B1112

To Lakenheath 2M

Lakenheath Station

Chicory Factory

Wilton Bridge
Head 3.3m

8.5m

Cut-off Channel

Cut-off Channel

Hockwold Hall

New Inn

Aqueduct

Sluice closed
at times of
flood
Gatehead 3m

Sluice open
at times of
flood

HOCKWOLD
CUM
WILTON

GS

Railway

N

Little Ouse River or Brandon Creek

Red
Lion
PH

Fenhouse Farm

Limekiln Farm

10.0m

10.0m

Woods

8.5m

Site of old Staunch

Mile 1

1 Kilometre (Approx)

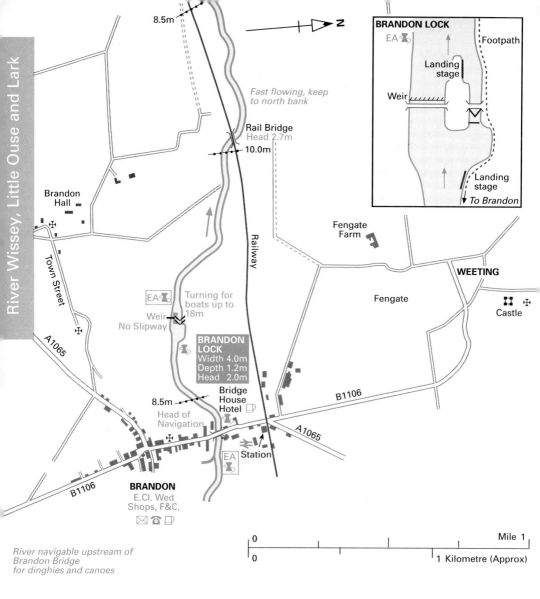

BRANDON LOCK

EA

Footpath

Landing stage

Weir

Landing stage

To Brandon

8.5m

N

Fast flowing, keep to north bank

Rail Bridge
Head 2.7m

10.0m

Railway

Brandon Hall

Fengate Farm

WEETING

Town Street

EA

Turning for boats up to 18m

Fengate

Castle

Weir
No Slipway

A1065

BRANDON LOCK
Width 4.0m
Depth 1.2m
Head 2.0m

Bridge House Hotel

B1106

8.5m

Head of Navigation

A1065

EA Station

B1106

BRANDON
E.Cl. Wed
Shops, F&C,

River navigable upstream of Brandon Bridge for dinghies and canoes

0				Mile 1
0			1 Kilometre (Approx)	

Immediately upstream from Wilton Bridge the river leaves, for a short distance, its natural bed which can still be traced by the rodhams lying along the county boundary, to flow in a concrete aqueduct across the cut-off channel and through the associated flood-relief sluices. Returning to its natural course, it leaves the flood banks behind and flows through a wide flood plain with a good riverside footpath crossing fields bordering the north bank. To the south it passes between three tumuli and, to the north, the site of a Romano-British villa lying at one end of the Foss Ditch, believed to be a 6th or 7th century Saxon defence. Running for some 10km between the rivers Little Ouse and Wissey, it starts at a small

creek on the north bank of the river on a bend very close to the Ely-to-Norwich railway.

The landscape now changes and the river becomes narrower, running between marshy fenland to the south and sandy warrens leading up to pine plantations in the north. It goes under a railway bridge (navigators use the northern of the two narrow channels) and, in quite a deep channel with a steep north bank, passes some ancient woodland to reach the new Brandon Lock, immediately downstream of which is a short length of Environment Agency moorings.

A short stretch then leads to the Breckland town of Brandon.

Brandon and Weeting

Although an old town built of local flint, its character has recently been much changed. To the north of the river is the railway line and a sizeable industrial estate. To the south are areas of unit-type small factories and businesses and large housing estates including one of some 140 bungalows built to cater for GLC overspill. The two large airfields at Mildenhall and Lakenheath have also had an impact on the town.

However, on the riverside by the road bridge are a number of hotels and attractive Georgian houses. To the north is the red-brick Georgian Brandon House Hotel, formerly the home of a prominent furrier. Opposite are the 14th century Ram Hotel (restaurant, bar food, bed and breakfast) and the riverside Bridge House Hotel (restaurant, bed and breakfast, mooring for patrons and rowing-boat hire). There is a public slipway on the north bank immediately upstream of the road bridge. South of the river behind the white-brick Connaught House, formerly the Chequers Inn, is Riverside Lodge Hotel.

Broad Street, the main shopping street, leads to Market Hill, the Flintknapper's Arms pub and the red-brick, Gothic-style school, clock tower and master's house built in 1878. At the end of Victoria Avenue, lined with fine pollarded limes is St Peter's Parish Church. Built on a pre-Norman site, some 14th century work has survived the restoration of 1873. To the west of the church is the two-storey, 17th century flint and red-brick Brandon Hall.

Although 2km to the north of the river, Weeting near Grimes Graves (once an Anglo-Saxon settlement called Weotingas, meaning wet fields) is altogether more interesting. The 11th century Weeting Castle, rebuilt by Earl Warren, son-in-law of William the Conqueror, is moated and has a three-storey keep-like tower. It is maintained by English Heritage and is open to the public at any reasonable time. There are no remains of Bromhill Priory, an Augustinian Priory built in about 1220 and suppressed 300 years later. Neither are there any remains of Weeting Hall, once the home of a prominent Russian merchant, John Julius Angerstein whose collection of 38 paintings, sold at his death for £57,000, formed the nucleus of the National Gallery's art collection.

Weeting had two churches: the ruined All Saints, possibly dating from the 11th century, was destroyed when its tower collapsed in about 1700; the round-towered Parish Church of St Mary's, also dating from the 11th century and with a Norman font, was much restored in the mid-19th century.

Whilst the footpath on the north bank of the river continues, Brandon road bridge is presently at the limit of navigation.

The River Lark

Branch Bridge to Prickwillow

The River Lark rises in Suffolk at Bradfield Combust near Bury St Edmunds. It is joined by the River Linnet near Mildenhall and then flows westwards to join the River Ouse midway between Ely and Littleport at Branch Bridge. It is navigable from its junction with the Ouse to Jude's Ferry between Isleham and Mildenhall. There are drove roads and footpaths along both banks as far as Isleham after which a footpath continues on the north bank to Mildenhall. Thereafter access is somewhat limited. There are Environment Agency moorings on the south bank opposite Tom's Hole Farm and on the same bank near the road bridge at Prickwillow. There are GOBA moorings at the entrance to Isleham Marina.

For the first 1½km from Branch Bridge, the river runs in a straight artificial channel, possibly Roman, before joining the natural meandering course of the ancient River Ouse to reach Prickwillow. The name Prickwillow is derived from the 'pricks' or skewers made from local willows. To the west the village street follows the course of the ancient Ouse. The parish church of St Peter, built on piles, dates from 1868 and contains a beautiful 17th century white marble font that was originally in Ely Cathedral. A church bell also dates from the 17th century and again came from the Cathedral. Because of the high water table there is no graveyard. The vicarage on Mile End Road provides a good example of the consequences of fen drainage. It was originally built, presumably with its foundations on the underlying clay, with two steps leading to the front door; now there are nine and the old cellars are ground-floor rooms.

Whilst there are no amenities in the

Mile 1

1 Kilometre (Approx)

0

River Great Ouse
See page 20

River Great Ouse

To Littleport
1.5 miles

Branch Bridge
3.4m

A10

To Ely 4
miles

N

Pump House   8.5m

Toms Hole
Farm

EA-🛥   ✕   EA

10.0m

Second Drove

PADNAL FEN

River Lark

Folly Farm

Phillips Hill Drove

To Ely
3 miles

B1382

Railway

10.0m

PRICKWILLOW
No PH or shops

Rail Bridge
3.1m

EA-🛥🎣   10.0m

Road Bridge
3.0m

EA

Mile End

Mile End
Farm

Museum of
Fen Pumping
Engines

Blackwing Drove

FODDER FEN

Pump
House

Lark Engine
Farm

Shell
Farm

Spooners
Farm

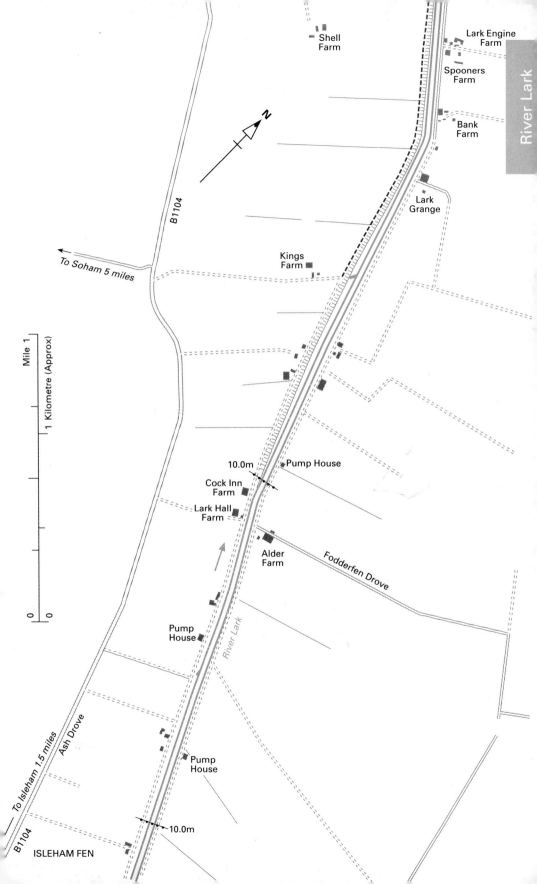

Shell Farm

Lark Engine Farm

Spooners Farm

Bank Farm

River Lark

N

B1104

Lark Grange

To Soham 5 miles

Kings Farm

Mile 1

1 Kilometre (Approx)

10.0m

Pump House

Cock Inn Farm

Lark Hall Farm

Alder Farm

Fodderfen Drove

0

River Lark

Pump House

To Isleham 1.5 miles

Ash Drove

B1104

Pump House

10.0m

ISLEHAM FEN

River Wissey, Little Ouse and Lark

ISLEHAM FEN

10.0m

10.0m

Delph Farm

B1104

10.0m

ISLEHAM FEN

ISLEHAM LOCK

To Isleham

Landing stage

Landing stage

GOBA

Isleham Marina

Fen Bank Road

Fenland Boats

Cooks Drove

Mile 1

1 Kilometre (Approx)

Elderberry Farm

Old Toll Ho

Mildenhall Speedway

8.5m

Hayland Drove

N

ISLEHAM LOCK
Width 4.55m
Depth 1.0m
Head 2.65m

Lock Keepers House

Waterside

Weir

GOBA

ISLEHAM MARINA
No petrol
☎ 01638 780663

Catchwater Farm

Fifty Farm

Chairfen Drove

To Isleham
1 mile
Public houses

Ferry Drove

C.H.
Spurgeon Memorial

EAST FEN

River Lark

Manor Farm

Thistley Green

Gravel Gardens

Lee Brook

Gravel Drove

0

0

Gravel
Gardens

Gravel Drove

**WEST
ROW**

E.Cl.Wed
GS ✉ ☎

Mildenhall
Airfield

Judes Ferry
House Inn
☎ 01638 712277

Current
Head of Navigation
Turning for boats
up to 13.7m

10.0m

Judes
Ferry
Bridge
Head 3.2m

Bargate
Farm

Hill Farm

River Lark (unnavigable)

Rectory
Farm

Footbridge
Kings
Staunch

To Fordham 3 miles

Chequers
PH
☎ 01638
713345

Wamil
Hall Farm

WORLINGTON

Road Bridge
19.3km

Mile 1

1 Kilometre (Approx)

B1102

MILDENHALL
Shops ✉ ☎

Mill

0

Barton Mills

village, there is a particularly interesting museum: the Prickwillow Drainage Engine Museum. The first steam engine here (dated 1831) was replaced by a beam steam engine in the 1880s. The engine house for that engine is the home of the present museum. In it are a number of old engines including a Vickers Petter two-cylinder, a three-cylinder Allen, and single-cylinder Ruston and Lister engines. The star attraction however is a five-cylinder Mirrlees Bickerton and Day Diesel dating from 1923 and capable of lifting 140 tons of water a minute. Whilst it was replaced in 1974 by a modern diesel engine, it remained as a standby until 1981–2. The museum is open for a small charge, daily in the summer and at weekends only in the winter. There are special 'run days' ☎ 01353 688360.

A local tale is told of a lady who had come from India to live near Prickwillow with a 'child' who appeared to be half human and half ape. The child was captured and taken to Cambridge but escaped, terrifying the local townsfolk. Although she was shot at and wounded, she managed to make her way home across the fen, killing those she met. She died after strangling the lady who had looked after her. No one goes near the old home as, on a misty night, two shadowy figures can be seen, one a lady, the other an ape with its arm around the lady's waist!

Prickwillow to Isleham

Leaving Prickwillow, the Lark flows northeast in the bed of an ancient stream before turning through 90° at Mile End. It continues high above the neighbouring fens in a long, straight, relatively featureless, embanked channel, probably improved during the period of monastic building and associated in particular with the building of the Abbey at Bury St Edmunds. It is bordered on the east bank in turn by a minor road, a drove road, a footpath and another drove road at Isleham Lock. Whilst there is a footpath along the whole of the west bank, access, other than at Prickwillow and Isleham, is somewhat limited.

On the northeast bank just beyond Mile End is another example of the consequences of fen drainage. Originally the ditches used to flow naturally into the Lark. However, as the fens were drained, first one then a second pumping station had to be built one

above the other. Today the water level in the drains is some 4 or 5m below the water level in the Lark.

Another pumping station with a diesel engine faces the Cock Inn Farm on the west bank. Earlier this century there were at least four pubs on this bank between Prickwillow and Isleham, no doubt catering for the lightermen.

At Fodder Fen, again on the east bank, is a third pumping station. On the wall of the engine house which dates from 1944 is a plaque with the following inscription:

To Joseph Flatt who had charge of this engine
from the date of its erection in 1844 to the day
of his death on April 21, 1900

Sadly the engine house is now empty.

At this point the metalled droveway leaves the east bank of the river and a footpath continues on the flood bank to the Old Toll House near Isleham Lock. It passes a pink, rendered, eight-sided, crooked building known locally as 'the Pepperpot'. Now privately owned it must be one of the few surviving examples of a former fenland windmill pump. Whilst lines of poplar trees now soften the severe fenland landscape, numerous pill-boxes are reminders of the nearby wartime airfields of Lakenheath and Mildenhall, currently used by the US Air Force.

After passing Fenland Boats with its private moorings, cruisers, barges and river homes, the character of the Lark changes at Elderberry Farm to that of a pleasant, natural, meandering river with a wide flood plain to the west. At Isleham Lock, a footpath leads to the medieval village of Isleham over a new 'cock-up' bridge at the entrance to Isleham Marina. Apart from a short stretch of GOBA moorings, the Marina with its waterside chalets and moorings is private. The path crosses the old River Lark, joining Waterside Road and Fen Bank to reach Isleham.

Isleham

Isleham is an ancient village with a unique atmosphere. Bronze-Age people lived here: the 'Isleham Hoard' of some 6,000 Bronze-Age artefacts, presently in the Moyses Hall Museum in Bury St Edmunds, is one of the largest of such hoards to be discovered in western Europe. Romans lived here: the remains of a Roman Villa have been unearthed. King Alfred granted a charter for the building of a chapel in 895 when the village was a Royal Manor known as Yselham.

It was an important medieval port with three quays, one on the triangle of land where Coates Drove joins Waterside, one where Coates Drove joins Pound Lane and one at Little London. Indeed Waterside, Coates Drove and the footpath around the Priory's fishponds to Little London mark the course of the original cut which joined the Lark to the three quays.

Its buildings are made of clunch, pebble, flint, ragstone, carstone, brick and concrete and range from medieval to modern. One of the oldest is the Benedictine Priory Church of St Margaret of Antioch, built in about 1090. Endowed with about 40ha it was given to the Benedictine Abbey of St Jacutus de Insula in Brittany. It was dissolved in 1414 and all that remains now, in the care of English Heritage, is a very rare example of a largely unaltered early Norman Chapel.

Behind a large lych-gate, known locally as 'the Stockhouse' after the small bay which once sheltered the village stocks, is the splendid Parish Church of St Andrew. Dating from 1320, it stands on the site of earlier Saxon and Norman Churches. Behind the door with its ancient 'Sanctuary Handle', it is full of treasures. Effigies date from 1275; the font is 14th century; one choir bench dates from around 1350 and there are bench-ends of about 1450; the hammer-beam roof, built in 1495, is enriched with ten downward-facing angels (there were originally 60); there is a large number of early brasses and elaborate monuments giving an insight to the fashionable dress and elegant attires of the 15th and 16th centuries; the eagle lectern is said to have been dug up from the fen in the 1870s.

Times were not always good for Isleham; it suffered from poverty and low living standards in the 1800s like many other fenland villages. In 1853 numerous people were reported as living in hollows; in one there were nearly 500. It is not surprising that there was a serious outbreak of cholera in this shanty town.

It is said there were once 27 pubs in Isleham; now there are three: the Griffin, the Sun and the Merry Monk. Dating from the 17th century, they all provide food. There is a garage, general store, small supermarket, post office, butcher and a fish and chip shop.

Isleham to Jude's Ferry

Continuing upstream, the straight artificial lock-cut rejoins the natural meandering River Lark to pass, on the south bank, a memorial tablet (accessible only across private land or by river) to a famous evangelist, the Reverend C Spurgeon:

> The Rev Charles
> Haddon Spurgeon
> The Prince of Preachers
> was baptised here on
> May 3 1850

For hundreds of years the river has been used for baptism by total immersion. First here, where there used to be a chain ferry whose ferry house doubled as the Ferry House Old Chair Public House and latterly near the weir at Isleham Marina. The practice ceased in 1970 due to the stagnant nature of the water and the consequent smell of those who had been baptised.

A pleasant, relatively wide stretch leads to Gravel Gardens, after which the river becomes significantly narrower with sharp bends and, at times, high banks. There is a footpath between Isleham and Jude's Ferry which, except for a short detour around Gravel Gardens, follows the north bank of the river from which, with luck, kingfishers, mink and even otters may be seen. There are several pill-boxes nearby one of which commands the final bend before Jude's Ferry Public House and road bridge.

West Row, a short walk away, is dominated by the neighbouring large and busy Mildenhall Airfield, and has little of interest nowadays. It does, however, have a history. Bargate Farm to the north of the river, is claimed by some to be on the site of the Anglo-Saxon Cloueshoh where synods were held annually from 673 with two of particular importance in 742 and 824. What is not in doubt however is that one of the greatest recent finds of treasure in the British Isles was made nearby in Thistley

Green in 1946. Deeper-than-usual ploughing of a nearby field uncovered a magnificent hoard of 34 pieces of late-Roman engraved and embossed silver dishes, goblets, bowls and spoons. Their amazing state of preservation reveals delicate engravings of Triton and Neptune as well as Bacchanalian friezes which include figures of Bacchus, Hercules and Pan. The find was declared Treasure Trove and is currently in the British Museum.

The present pub at Jude's Ferry (a Corruption of Judd and first called the Ferry), built on the site of a much older building, dates from 1849. It is a welcoming pub with a riverside garden, moorings for patrons and meals served in the bar or restaurant. Since it is only about 2km from the main runway of Mildenhall Airfield, where regular air displays are held, the display in May being the largest in Europe, Jude's Ferry is a popular spot from which to watch the flying, particularly amongst navigators; up to 44 boats have moored at the pub.

Whilst Jude's Ferry is the limit of navigation, the somewhat overgrown footpath from Isleham continues on the north bank as far as Mildenhall. Thereafter access is generally only by road.

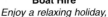

The River Cam and the Lodes

Oh, is the water sweet and cool,
Gentle and brown above the pool?
And laughs the immortal river still
Under the mill; under the mill?
Say, is there Beauty yet to find?
And Certainty? and Quiet kind?
Deep meadows yet, for to forget
The lies and truths and pains? Oh! yet
Stands the Church clock at ten to three
And is there honey still for tea?

Rupert Brooke

The River Cam

Pope's Corner to Upware

At Pope's Corner, the River Great Ouse divides to form the Rivers Cam and Old West. On the junction, the Fish and Duck restaurant and marina, under new ownership, have been extensively restored. ☎ 01353 649580 (moorings for patrons). The River Cam continues southwards in a wide meandering channel. Lying between the river and the western floodbank are the Wicken Washes, low-lying land which is often naturally flooded, rich in birdlife, including, shelduck, oyster catchers, swans, Canada geese, curlew, grebe, snipe and tufted duck. Before reaching the concrete 1930s Dimmock's Cote road bridge, built on the site of an old ferry crossing, there are small osier beds on either side of the river.

To the west, between the Rivers Cam and Old West, lies some of the most fertile black fen soil in which is grown one of the largest celery crops in the United Kingdom. To the east the land rises slightly and cretaceous beds rich with small marine fossils, overlying gault clay where ammonites can be found, supply a lime works.

Proceeding upstream under the road bridge and past the GOBA moorings on the east bank towards Upware, the river becomes less confined. There are no flood banks on the east and those to the west are occasionally well set back. The Second World War pill box is at the outfall of the Waterbeach Internal Drainage Board pumping station, built in 1945. Upware Marina is private but supplies diesel and workshop facilities (not available for hirecraft). For patrons there are extensive moorings along the pleasant frontage of the neighbouring public house, Five Miles from Anywhere, No Hurry Inn, rebuilt in 1980 some time after the previous inn was destroyed by fire in 1957.

Upware has had a colourful past. In the 1850s the celebrated Upware Republic was founded by a university club at the Five Miles from Anywhere, No Hurry Inn (formerly the Lord Nelson) with a president, a consul, a treasurer, a justice, its own laws and its own money. However not only was there a republic but in the 1870s, Richard Fielder MA, Member of Lincoln's Inn, proclaimed himself King of Upware. Dressed habitually in a scarlet waistcoat and corduroy breeches, he spent much of this time drinking from his own six-gallon jug of punch known as His Majesty's Pint and fighting and arguing with bargees. Other university clubs to have met at Upware include the Idiots and the Beersoakers.

Early in the 19th century, the Inn was the regular haunt of a local farmer, Hempsall. One night he set off in a thick fog to his home across the fen which he knew well. The fog lasted for three days and nothing was heard of Hempsall. When the fog cleared, a group of farmers set out to find him. On their way Hempsall appeared walking towards them saying that he had lost his life on the first day of the fog. He told them where his body would be found lying in the slime and mud and he asked to be buried at Wicken. His body was found as he had said but he was taken to Soham where he was buried. He is said to still haunt the fen and will not rest until he is buried at Wicken.

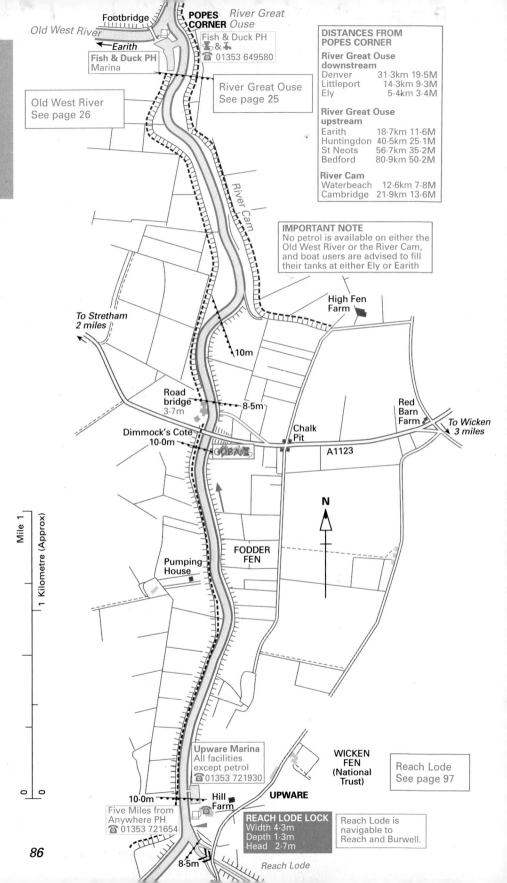

Footbridge **POPES CORNER** *River Great Ouse*

Old West River

←*Earith*

Fish & Duck PH
Marina

Fish & Duck PH
🍴 & ⚓
☎ 01353 649580

River Great Ouse
See page 25

Old West River
See page 26

DISTANCES FROM POPES CORNER

River Great Ouse downstream
Denver	31·3km	19·5M
Littleport	14·3km	9·3M
Ely	5·4km	3·4M

River Great Ouse upstream
Earith	18·7km	11·6M
Huntingdon	40·5km	25·1M
St Neots	56·7km	35·2M
Bedford	80·9km	50·2M

River Cam
Waterbeach	12·6km	7·8M
Cambridge	21·9km	13·6M

River Cam

IMPORTANT NOTE
No petrol is available on either the Old West River or the River Cam, and boat users are advised to fill their tanks at either Ely or Earith

High Fen Farm

To Stretham 2 miles

10m

Road bridge
3·7m
8·5m

Dimmock's Cote
10·0m

GOBA

Chalk Pit

Red Barn Farm

To Wicken 3 miles

A1123

N

FODDER FEN

Pumping House

Mile 1

1 Kilometre (Approx)

Upware Marina
All facilities except petrol
☎ 01353 721930

WICKEN FEN (National Trust)

Reach Lode
See page 97

10·0m

Hill Farm

UPWARE

Five Miles from Anywhere PH
☎ 01353 721654

REACH LODE LOCK
Width 4·3m
Depth 1·3m
Head 2·7m

Reach Lode is navigable to Reach and Burwell.

8·5m

Reach Lode

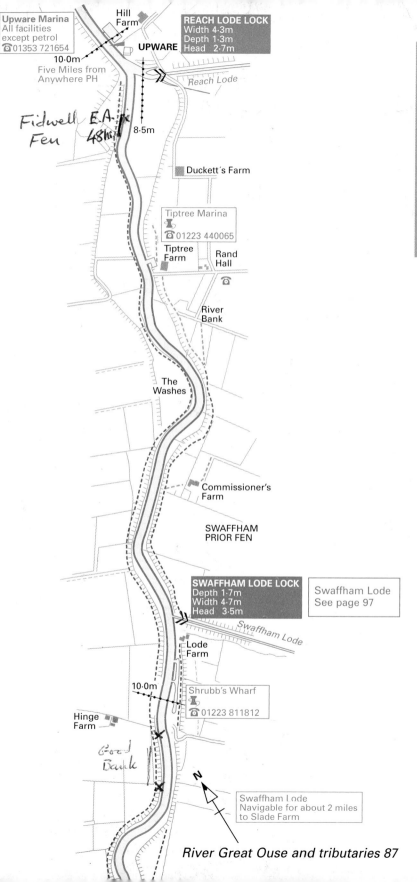

Upware Marina
All facilities
except petrol
☎ 01353 721654

Hill
Farm

REACH LODE LOCK
Width 4·3m
Depth 1·3m
Head 2·7m

UPWARE

10·0m
Five Miles from
Anywhere PH

Reach Lode

Fidwell E.A. k
Fen 48hr

8·5m

Duckett's Farm

Tiptree Marina
☎ 01223 440065

Tiptree
Farm

Rand
Hall

☎

River
Bank

The
Washes

Commissioner's
Farm

SWAFFHAM
PRIOR FEN

SWAFFHAM LODE LOCK
Depth 1·7m
Width 4·7m
Head 3·5m

Swaffham Lode
See page 97

Swaffham Lode

Lode
Farm

10·0m

Shrubb's Wharf
☎ 01223 811812

Hinge
Farm

Good
Bank

N

Swaffham Lode
Navigable for about 2 miles
to Slade Farm

River Great Ouse and tributaries 87

Mile 1

1 Kilometre (Approx)

0

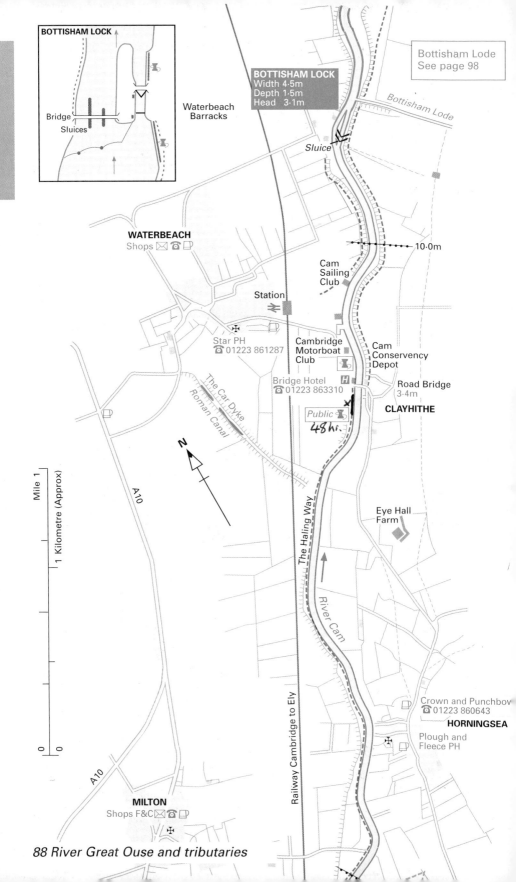

BOTTISHAM LOCK

Bridge
Sluices

Waterbeach
Barracks

Bottisham Lode
See page 98

Bottisham Lode

BOTTISHAM LOCK
Width 4·5m
Depth 1·5m
Head 3·1m

Sluice

10·0m

WATERBEACH
Shops ✉ ☎ ⌷

Cam
Sailing
Club

Station

Star PH
☎ 01223 861287

Cambridge
Motorboat
Club

Cam
Conservency
Depot

Road Bridge
3·4m

Bridge Hotel
☎ 01223 863310

CLAYHITHE

Public
48 hr.

The Car Dyke

Roman Canal

N

Eye Hall
Farm

Mile 1

1 Kilometre (Approx)

A10

The Haling Way

River Cam

0

Crown and Punchbowl
☎ 01223 860643

HORNINGSEA

Plough and
Fleece PH

Railway Cambridge to Ely

A10

MILTON
Shops F&C ✉ ☎ ⌷

88 River Great Ouse and tributaries

Upware to Bottisham Lock

The lock on the east bank marks the entrance to Reach Lode. See page 94. Before long the western flood bank becomes well set back and the wash land between the river and this bank is often flooded for wildfowling. Again this area is rich in birdlife and, if one is lucky, both marsh and hen harriers can be seen.

Between a small private marina on the east bank at Tiptree Farm and Bottisham Lock some 4km upstream, the river becomes somewhat featureless running in a relatively high banked channel with, at times, flood banks very close, particularly on the west side. Swaffham Bulbeck Lode enters the river from the east at a lock with pointing doors and a guillotine gate close to some private off-river moorings. Bottisham Lode also joins the river from the east through single pointing doors opposite a Second World War pill box and a short length of private moorings.

To the west lies Waterbeach, whose railway station is close to the river. Near the station to the south are the remaining earthworks of the Norman Waterbeach Abbey for Franciscan Nuns. A little further south is a short stretch of the Roman Carr Dyke, part of a canal and river system which linked Cambridge with Lincoln. To the north near the station was an old dock which was connected directly to the river by a short lode.

Waterbeach, once described as 'a Fenne town of large extent . . . having large and spacious commons and marsh grounds as most of the fen towns have, which is the cause that a multitude of poor and mean people do inhabit there, to live an easy and idle life, by Fishing, Fowling and Feeding of Cattle', has a number of fine 16th and 17th century properties and its church of St John, whilst much rebuilt, dates from 1200. The nearby airfield, completed in 1941, has been used variously for bombers, fighters, training, transport command and, after flying ceased in the 1960s, by RAF Construction and, latterly, the Royal Engineers.

North of the airfield and at some distance from the river are the remains of Denny Abbey which was founded as a cell of Ely in 1160 by monks driven out of an earlier establishment at Elmeney by frequent flooding. In about 1180 Ely handed the site to the Knights Templars. After their suppression in the early 13th century, the Abbey was given to the Countess of Pembroke and she received the Poor Clares from the Franciscan Abbey in the south of the village.

The remains, partly incorporated into later stone-built buildings, are believed to be the only example of an early monastic foundation being converted for the use of Franciscans. They are cared for by English Heritage and are open to the public during the summer between 10am and 6pm (except lunch-times).

To continue walking alongside the river, cross it at the lock and continue on the east bank as far as Clayhithe before re-crossing at the road bridge onto the west bank.

Immediately up stream of the lock the character of the river changes dramatically for the better and particular features are the sailing boats of the River Cam Sailing Club. Both this club and the neighbouring Cambridge Motor Boat Club are set in well-kept grounds with attractive wooden chalets.

Bottisham Lock to Fen Ditton

Leaving Bottisham Lock, where the responsibility for navigation transfers from the Environment Agency to the Cam Conservancy, the River Cam passes the private Cam Sailing Club and Cambridge Motor Boat Club to reach Clayhithe. A ferry existed here from the early 14th century until the 1870s and Clayhithe was once the popular destination of a traditional August bank holiday excursion from Cambridge by steam launch. The Bridge Hotel (moorings for patrons) is opposite the large 19th century yellow-brick Conservators' House with its Dutch gable ends. Formerly containing the Conservators' board room, it is currently their foreman's home.

Passing under Clayhithe Bridge, the Haling Way, the old tow-path on the west bank, is the only footpath along the river to Cambridge. Whilst there is no public mooring on this stretch of the river until Jubilee Gardens in Cambridge, the Conservancy permits short, overnight stops. After a brief open stretch near where the Car Dyke must have joined the Cam, the river passes through a dark, gloomy and rather quiet length with tall ivy-clad trees before opening out again to give a view of Horningsea and St Peter's Church, parts of

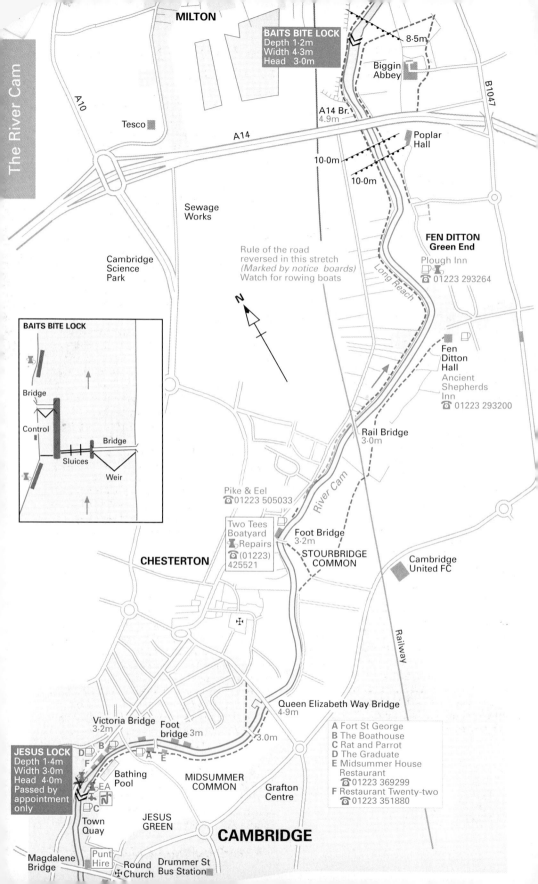

MILTON

BAITS BITE LOCK
Depth 1·2m
Width 4·3m
Head 3·0m

8·5m

Biggin Abbey

B1047

A10

Tesco

A14

A14 Br. 4·9m

Poplar Hall

10·0m

10·0m

Sewage Works

FEN DITTON
Green End

Plough Inn
☎ 01223 293264

Cambridge Science Park

Rule of the road
reversed in this stretch
(Marked by notice boards)
Watch for rowing boats

Long Reach

N

Fen Ditton Hall
Ancient Shepherds Inn
☎ 01223 293200

BAITS BITE LOCK

Bridge

Control

Bridge

Sluices

Weir

Rail Bridge
3·0m

Pike & Eel
☎ 01223 505033

River Cam

Two Tees
Boatyard
Repairs
☎ (01223)
425521

Foot Bridge
3·2m

**STOURBRIDGE
COMMON**

Cambridge
United FC

CHESTERTON

Railway

Queen Elizabeth Way Bridge
4·9m

Victoria Bridge
3·2m

Foot bridge 3m

3·0m

A Fort St George
B The Boathouse
C Rat and Parrot
D The Graduate
E Midsummer House
   Restaurant
   ☎ 01223 369299
F Restaurant Twenty-two
   ☎ 01223 351880

JESUS LOCK
Depth 1·4m
Width 3·0m
Head 4·0m
Passed by
appointment
only

D
B
F
A E

EA

C

Bathing Pool

**MIDSUMMER
COMMON**

Grafton
Centre

**JESUS
GREEN**

Town Quay

CAMBRIDGE

Magdalene
Bridge

Punt
Hire

Round
Church

Drummer St
Bus Station

which date from the 13th century. A settlement has been in existence here since the Iron Age and the present church replaces a much bigger Saxon 'minster' church which had a large community of secular canons in the 9th century. The only access to the village, difficult from the river, is along a small lane between a modern bungalow with its line of ten magnificent weeping willows and an orchard. The lane once served lighters bringing coal for a thriving brick industry and returning with the bricks. In the village are the Plough and Fleece and Crown and Punch Bowl public houses (meals) and a large garden centre.

There are private moorings to the north and a small private marina to the south opposite which is an unusual seat carved out of an old fallen willow tree. The fully automated Baits Bite lock is reached after passing a lane on the west bank which leads to the largely urbanised village of Milton. For the next few hundred metres the river is dominated by the road bridge carrying the A14, now one of the busiest roads in the country. Just before passing through the bridge, Biggin Abbey can be glimpsed to the east. The cement rendering hides a late 14th century building that never was an abbey; it was the summer residence of the Bishops of Ely. Rules of the road may be reversed along this length of river.

The upstream side of the bridge is daubed with the graffiti of various Cambridge University boat clubs and indeed, for the next 3km, the river is home to rowing races. The most well known of these are the University 'Bumps': the 'Lents' held just before Easter and the 'Mays' held at the beginning of June. Within Divisions, boats set off at regular intervals, the tow-path crowded with their frenzied supporters, with the objective of catching the boat in front and actually touching it (that is 'bumping' it). The next day the boat which made the 'bump' starts in front of the one which it 'bumped' and so on. At other times of the year there are more traditional races in which the boats are timed over the course. A popular place to watch the racing is from the Plough public house at Fen Ditton.

Fen Ditton to Jesus Lock, Cambridge

Fen Ditton with its thatched cottages and elegant 16th and 17th century houses with graceful terraced lawns sweeping down the river, is at the end of the northern part of the pre-Saxon Fleam Dyke. The Hall, built in 1635 around a medieval timbered house, provides a fine example of old red brickwork with Dutch gables. There is more red brickwork on the lovely front of the early 18th century Old Vicarage. The church of St Mary, whilst dating from the 14th century was rebuilt in 1887. Sadly the famous traditional afternoon teas can no longer be taken on the riverside lawns of the Barn, the thatched house next to the Plough Inn. Other pubs in the village include the Ancient Shepherds, the Kings Head and the Blue Lion.

A story is told of a local gardener and a former sexton who, in 1847, made drunken and libellous statements about the chastity of the rector's wife. Two years later he was sentenced to pay costs and do penance. On the due day, 3,000 people turned up, some with reserved seats which were already occupied by a noisy, disreputable crowd that spilled all over the church, its chancel, the capitals of the pillars and even onto the roof. As he attempted to make his penance, a riot broke out; pews were broken, windows smashed and hassocks thrown. When he had finished the crowd went on to the rectory, where nearly every window was smashed, before returning for the rest of the day to the Plough.

After a bend in the river there is a rather ugly view of the gasworks and an iron lattice railway bridge. Upstream and to the north is Chesterton, with its two popular riverside pubs, the Tudor Green Dragon and on the river's edge under chestnut trees where the tow-path finishes, the Pike and Eel. Once home to the rough watermen of the Cam whose horses had to wade upstream through the river towing their lighters to the public quays in Cambridge, Chesterton is now a suburb of the city. Among the lanes there are some fine buildings including the mid-14th century Chesterton Tower, the former residence of the proctor of the Canons Regular of Vercelli near Turin, the red-brick Jacobean Chesterton Hall with its Dutch gables, and St Andrew's Church dating from the early 14th century, on whose bench ends are rare carved human figures (c.1420–30).

The houses soon give way to the many college boathouses which line the north bank to Victoria Bridge and beyond. Opposite is the open ground of Stourbridge Common, the former site of one of the greatest fairs in Europe, Stourbridge Fair. It started in King John's reign and, in nearby Barnwell, the Leper Hospital of St Mary Magdalene, whose disused Norman Chapel still remains, received its tolls. Lasting for three weeks from 7 September, Defoe describes how no less than 50 hackney coaches came from London; Sir Isaac Newton bought his three famous prisms there; there was a cheese fair, a hop fair, a booksellers row; a cooks row; Baltic timber, Italian silks and Spanish iron could be bought. On the edge of the common, two streets – Garlic Row and Oyster Row – are the only legacy of this great fair.

After a group of house boats, the land to the south opens out again into Midsummer Common where the annual Strawberry Fair and the vast mid-summer fair are held. Passing another popular riverside inn, the Fort St George, the River Cam flows under Victoria Road bridge to reach Jesus Green and the limit of navigation, Jesus Green Lock.

Cambridge by river

To see Cambridge by river, take a punt, perhaps chauffeured, from Magdalene Bridge and punt upstream under Magdalene Bridge along the 'Backs' of the colleges with their beautiful gardens and lawns. The traditional Cambridge style is to stand on the platform as opposed to standing in the punt, the traditional Oxford style. Beware of catching the punt pole on one of the many low bridges or getting it stuck in the mud. A quick twist of the pole will usually free it from the mud but, if in doubt, let go!

The first college is St John's with its two bridges, the 19th century Bridge of Sighs and the Old Bridge designed by Wren and built in 1712. Round a bend in the river is a second Wren building, The Great Wren Library of Trinity College built in the late 17th century. After Trinity Bridge and Garret Hostel Bridge, where the small lane is the last of many which ran down from the city to hythes on the river, is the best known bridge of all the bridges on the 'Backs', Clare College Bridge dating from 1640 with its beautiful stone balls. When asked how

many there are, examine them carefully before replying. The broad sweeping lawns of King's College provide the perfect foreground to King's College Chapel and the Gibbs' Building. After King's College bridge is the Mathematical Bridge of Queen's College, a 1902 copy of James Essex's bridge, built in 1749 without nails and using just wooden pegged timbers.

The 'Backs' come to a sudden end at the very busy Silver Street Bridge where the Cam enters the Mill Pond with its popular boat yards and pubs.

For those with time to spare, take a punt from the boatyard above the weir, under the ugly modern University Centre, and go upstream past the elegant lawns of the Garden House Hotel through open countryside to Grantchester and afternoon tea in the Orchards.

Cambridge on foot

There is probably no other city in the world where such a variety of architecture can be seen on a walk of little more than a kilometre. Starting at Magdalene Bridge, half-timbered houses are passed before reaching the 12th century Round Church of St Sepulchre, now a brass-rubbing centre. Turning down Trinity Street, past St John's College Tudor gateway, the 16th century Great Gate of Trinity College with its statue of Henry VIII usually holding – instead of a sceptre – a chair leg, the Victorian front of Gonville and Caius College (generally called Caius and pronounced 'Keys') opposite which is St Michael's Church dating from 1327 (currently used for community work), the early 18th century Senate House, where degrees are conferred and the Old Schools dating from 1347, King's Parade is reached.

Opposite the Senate House is the University Church of Great St Mary, parts of which date from the 13th century and from whose tower is one of the best views of Cambridge. King's College with its world-famous Tudor chapel fronts King's Parade. On the other side of the road, Bene't Street leads to the Tourist Information Office after passing the beautifully restored Eagle Pub with its early wall paintings, panelled rooms, stone floors and American Bar on whose ceiling American wartime airmen wrote their names and squadron numbers. Opposite is the oldest church in Cambridge, the Saxon Church of St Bene't (short for St

Benedict), dating from about 1000.

Trumpington Street starts at the junction of King's Parade and Bene't Street and passes between St Catherine's College founded in 1473 and Corpus Christi College founded 120 years earlier. Before Fitzbillies, a cake shop known to all undergraduates, opposite the red-brick Cambridge University Press buildings (1831), is St Botolph's Church with Norman fragments in the tower. Mill Lane, opposite Downing Street, leads to the riverside Garden House Hotel. Across Downing Street is Pembroke College, founded in 1347, and opposite is the oldest college in Cambridge, Peterhouse, founded in 1280. At the end of the walk are two contrasting buildings, the monumental Fitzwilliam Museum with its great and varied treasures and, on the other side of the road, the ultra-modern façade of the recently restored Old Addenbrooke's Hospital.

The Cambridgeshire Lodes

The medieval word for a waterway was Lode and the Cambridgeshire Lodes – Soham, Wicken, Burwell, Reach, Swaffham and Bottisham – form a unique network of waterways joining the River Cam with villages lying to the east on the edge of the chalk uplands. Whilst some suggest they were dug as boundary markers and others that they were built as a series of defences across the fen, the Devil's Ditch being an extension of one Lode, on balance they are all believed to originally have been Roman transport canals. Whilst their heyday was in the 17th and 18th centuries, their use declined rapidly with the coming of the railway in 1884. Today they are preserved in embanked channels conveying water from the chalk uplands across the lower lying fenland. Wicken, Burwell, Reach and part of Swaffham Lode are still navigable but only for small, narrower craft.

Soham Lode

Beyond Barway, at the head of the longest lode, Soham was once a lakeside settlement beside Soham Mere, a large inland lake drained in the second half of the 18th century. No trace remains of the monastery established in 631 and destroyed by the Danes in the 12th century. It was here that the first Bishop of East Anglia, St Felix, was initially buried before being removed to Ramsey Abbey. It is said that a boat race for his bones was held on the mere between the monks of Ramsey and Ely! The parish church of St John dates from the 12th century and its churchyard is on the site of a pagan East Anglian cemetery.

A memorial in the church commemorates how, in June 1944, Soham was saved from almost certain total destruction when the driver of a 51-wagon ammunition train noticed that the first wagon was on fire. Together with his fireman they uncoupled the wagon and tried to pull it through the station into open country. However after a few hundred meters, it exploded, killing the fireman and a nearby signalman, severely injuring the driver, wrecking the station and damaging over 750 houses some up to half a mile away. The shock was felt for over 20 miles around.

Soham is now a straggling village some 3km long with a number of fine Georgian houses. The thatched Red Lion public house is in the centre alongside shops, banks and restaurants.

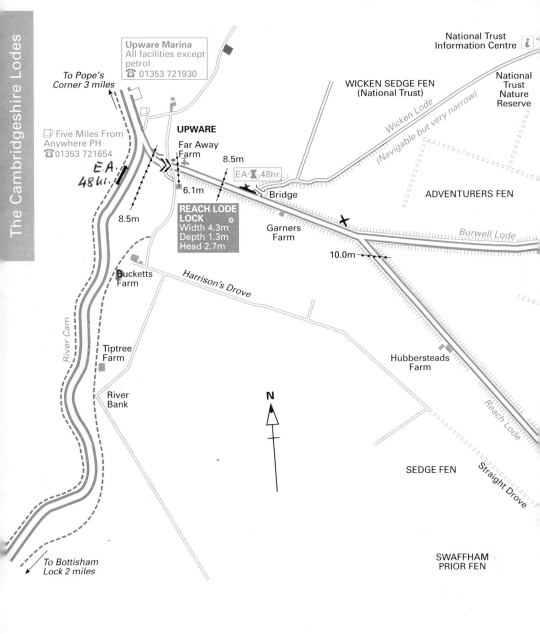

Reach Lode	
Upware to Reach village	
Distance	4.8km (3 miles)
Length	15.2m (50')
Beam	4.1m (13' 6")
Draught	0.8m (2' 7")
Headroom	2.7m (8' 10")
Locks	1

Reach Lode and Burwell Lode	
Upware, junction with the River Cam, to Burwell village	
Distance	6.1km (3.8 miles)
Length	15.2m (50')
Beam	4.1m (13' 6")
Draught	1.2m (4')
Headroom	2.7m (8' 10")
Locks	1

94 River Great Ouse and tributaries

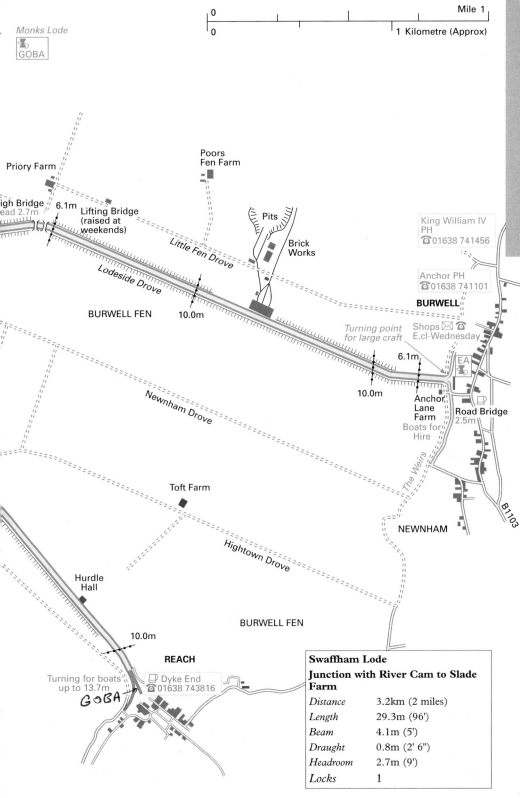

Monks Lode
GOBA

0 — Mile 1
0 — 1 Kilometre (Approx)

Priory Farm

Poors
Fen Farm

igh Bridge
ead 2.7m

6.1m

Lifting Bridge
(raised at
weekends)

Little Fen Drove

Pits

Brick
Works

King William IV
PH
☎01638 741456

Anchor PH
☎01638 741101

BURWELL

Lodeside Drove

BURWELL FEN

10.0m

Turning point
for large craft

Shops ✉ ☎
E.cl-Wednesday

6.1m

10.0m

Anchor
Lane
Farm

Boats for
Hire

EA

Road Bridge
2.5m

Newnham Drove

The Weirs

NEWNHAM

B1103

Toft Farm

Hightown Drove

Hurdle
Hall

BURWELL FEN

10.0m

REACH

Turning for boats
up to 13.7m

GOBA

Dyke End
☎01638 743816

Swaffham Lode	
Junction with River Cam to Slade Farm	
Distance	3.2km (2 miles)
Length	29.3m (96')
Beam	4.1m (5')
Draught	0.8m (2' 6")
Headroom	2.7m (9')
Locks	1

River Great Ouse and tributaries 95

Wicken Lode

Continuing upstream beyond Reach Lode
Lock, a wooden 'cock up' bridge on the
north bank marks the entrance to the
narrow Wicken Lode leading to Wicken Fen
and Wicken village. The Lode is navigable
for about 1¼km, Wicken village a further
walk of about 1½km. Wicken Fen is one of
the country's best-known, oldest nature
reserves, the first tract of land being
purchased by the National Trust in 1899.
Today the Trust manages 297ha of
wetland; a naturalist's paradise rich in
plants, insects and birds. Whilst it is neither
a 'true' fen standing as it does above the
surrounding long-drained land, nor a relic
of natural ancient fenland, it has a spirit of
its own described by Edward Storey as
'timeless, solitary, proud, almost
aristocratic'. Nature trails and a boardwalk
start at the Warden's office (where there is a
comprehensive display describing the
history and management of the fen) and
pass the last surviving drainage windmill
pump reassembled from Adventurers Fen in
1956, now used in reverse to help maintain
the wetland. The reserve is open throughout
the year and a traditional fenland cottage,
furnished as it would have been in the
1930s is open on Sunday and bank holiday
Monday afternoons.

North of the fen is Spinney Abbey,
originally the small priory of St Mary and
the Holy Cross, founded by the Count of
Brittany's great grand-daughter in 1215 on
land which the family had owned since
1086. For the most part there was only a
prior and three canons. However they may
not have been isolated because, according
to legend, a secret passage led from Spinney
Abbey to Denny Abbey the other side of the
river and home to the Poor Clares, well-to-
do Franciscan nuns. It fell into private
hands in about 1530 and was owned for a
time by one of Oliver Cromwell's sons,
Henry. The present stone-built farmhouse
incorporating parts of the old Abbey, dates
from 1775 and is said to be haunted: could
it be by a prior who was murdered in 1403
by three of his own canons?

In the Parish Church of St Laurence,
dating from the 13th century, there is a
memorial to Henry Cromwell and his
family. In the village there is a restored
smock grain mill, blacksmith and the
thatched Maids Head public house
(restaurant and bar meals).

Burwell Lode

A short distance beyond the 'cock up'
bridge, the Lode divides: Burwell Lode to
the north and Reach Lode continuing
south. Passing the former works where pale
yellow local bricks were made, Burwell
Lode reaches Burwell after a further 4km.
Here, at the limit of navigation, where there
is a turning point for long craft, the Lode
divides again and once served canals,
basins, wharves and warehouses at the
bottom of narrow plots of land leading from
the merchants' houses, all built gable-end to
the street. A small lane beside the Anchor
public house (bar meals) with its lode-side
garden, leads into the village.

It started probably as a collection of
Roman and later Saxon settlements.
Burwell means 'Spring by the Fort' and
indeed there are still springs below the west
end of St Mary's churchyard close by the
ruins of Burwell Castle, built by King
Stephen on the site of an earlier Roman
fortification. The castle was one of a series
built in about 1134 by the King as defences
against a rebellion led by Geoffry de
Mandeville. Whilst it was being constructed
it was actually attacked by Geoffry, who was
killed in the battle. The rebellion collapsed,
there was no need for the castle and it was
never completed.

The large flint and clunch church of St
Mary, possibly Saxon and Norman in
origin, is a fine example of early-English
perpendicular style. There are similarities in
style with King's College Chapel and
Queen's College Gatehouse in Cambridge;
possibly they all had the same architect.
Commemorated here is an event that
occurred in September 1778, when over 80
people were burnt to death while watching a
travelling puppet show on its way to
Stourbridge Fair in Cambridge. The doors
had been locked and nailed up – ostensibly
to keep more people from joining an already
full show – but possibly, in reality, by a man
with a grudge against the show.

The village has a number of fine ancient
buildings and, next to the windmill, is a
small museum with domestic and rural
bygones. The plentiful amenities include a
number of pubs (bar meals), a Chinese
takeaway, a butcher, two bakers, a chemist,
a post office, a Co-op, a newsagent and a
Barclays Bank.

Reach Lode

The small ancient village of Reach lies at the end of Reach Lode a distance of about 3½km from its junction with Burwell Lode and at the start of the Devil's Dyke. Passing over the higher chalk uplands, the Roman Devil's Dyke, with its 5½m high rampart and 4½m deep, 6m wide ditch, continues for some 11km into Suffolk. Here rare plants can be found including the pasque flower (anemone pulsatilla). Originally the Dyke passed through the middle of the village down to the Lode. However, in about 1750, it was levelled to form the present village green and the small artificial promontory dividing Reach Lode into two narrow waterways which then lead to six or seven small basins at the back of merchants' houses.

From its origins in the Iron Age, the village developed rapidly in early medieval times as a trading station with docks for sea-going ships. Reach's importance was reflected in the tradition which said that, whilst Cambridge was a village, Reach was a city with up to nine churches. It was also claimed that at midday on 8 January 1201, King John signed a charter giving it its freedom for ever. With the coming of the railway, however, its trade declined rapidly, the last commercial load being carried in the 1930s.

Today, whilst an electricity sub-station has been built on the promontory, a number of fine houses remain, including the Manor House parts of which date from the 16th century. The ruins of the one and only original church, dedicated to St Etheldreda, lie behind the present typically Victorian church. There is a small inn, Dyke End, on the north of the green.

Reach still maintains an important link with the past through its annual fair dating possibly from the 10th century and which was also given a charter by King John. It was always held during Rogation Week and was opened by the Mayor and Corporation of Cambridge who threw pennies to the crowds both on the way to and at the fair. More recently the date has been changed to that of the May bank holiday because it is said that, due to the flexible date of Rogation Week, some years one Mayor could open two fairs during his term of office, whilst in other years there might be no fair for the Mayor of the time to open.

Swaffham Bulbeck Lode

Swaffham Bulbeck Lode, navigable to Slade Farm, leads directly across remote fenland to Commercial End, situated between Swaffham Bulbeck and Swaffham Prior a distance of about 5½km but is only navigable for about 2½km to Slades Farm. As its name implies this was the business end of the Lode, an inland port founded on important river trade which had started in Roman times and where sea-going vessels docked throughout the Middle Ages. There are a number of fine buildings including Abbey House, built in 1778 above the vaulted 13th century undercroft of a small priory of Benedictine nuns, the late 17th century Merchants House, Lordship House, a water mill and maltings, parts of which are claimed to date from 1697.

To the north, Swaffham Prior is famous for its two churches in one church yard. In the 11th century the village was owned in equal parts by the Prior of Ely, a gentleman called Hardwin de Scalers and three knights of the court of Count Alan of Brittany. One church, St Mary's probably belonged to Ely, whilst the other, dedicated to St Cyriac (or Cyr) and St Julitta, a mother and son martyred early in the 4th century, may have belonged to the French knights, St Cyr being highly venerated in France. Whilst the two churches became united in 1667, St Cyr was in ruins by 1800 and in spite of being rebuilt, with the exception of the 15th century octagon tower, it was in ruins again by the 1970s. St Mary's had a remarkable five-stage tower; first square Norman, second octagonal Norman, third and fourth 13th century sixteen-sided and fifth a 14th century spire. The spire was struck by lightning in 1767 and destroyed. The nave was damaged and, like its neighbour, the church fell into disrepair. It is now however completely refurbished and has some interesting brasses.

In the main street are a number of fine, early houses including the half-timbered Tudor Baldwin Manor, which may have links with the French knights, Knights Hall, Anglesey House, the Manor House, Swaffham Prior House and the Red Lion public house (bar meals except Mondays). Overlooking the village an unsympathetic water tower separates a tower windmill, which is still used to grind flour, and a smock windmill.

Opposite Swaffham Bulbeck's 13th century church, also dedicated to St Mary, are some half-timbered houses. At the southern end of the village is the 15th century timbered Burgh Hall which may have been the estate house of the French Bolbec family who settled in the area in the middle of the 11th century and who gave the village its name.

There is a tale in the village of the sale of a wife by public auction at the former Royal Oak Inn. The lady, the wife of one of two tinkers, was led into the auction room by a halter tied round her neck and made to stand on a footstool. She was described as being a most desirable lot 'with a red nose, thick lips, bent back, receding chin and eyes of which one looks straight at you, the other wanders up to the North'. Bidding started at sixpence and she was eventually bought by the other tinker for half-a-crown.

In the middle of the village is the Black Horse public house (bar meals) and a post office and small store.

Bottisham Lode

Bottisham Lode, now shallow and not navigable, was once a busy waterway serving not only the village of Lode, the inland port for Bottisham, but also leading into Quy Water and thence to the village of Quy (a corruption of Cow Island), where remains of medieval moorings can still be found in farm walls. Much trade was conducted at the white weather-boarded mill lying between the Lode and Quy Water and at which, following full restoration to working order by the National Trust, fresh stone-ground flour can be purchased during demonstrations on the first Saturday of each month.

Unlike Commercial End, there is little in Lode to reflect its former prosperity. Other than a few 17th century buildings, its church of St James and the majority of properties are 19th century. However Lode is neighbour to the beautiful Anglesey Abbey.

Anglesey, derived either from the Saxon tribal name for the island where Angles Live or, equally appropriately, as a corruption of Angersale meaning a grassy nook, has been inhabited since the 5th century. The Abbey, an Augustine Priory founded in 1135 and substantially rebuilt a hundred years later, fell under the Act for the Suppression of Smaller Monasteries in 1536. In about 1600, the Chapter House was converted into a domestic dwelling. Whilst the present Abbey results from significant restoration,

alteration and rebuilding in 1861 and 1926, it still retains the original prior's chamber overlying an undercroft and what is believed to be the hall of the priors and their guests.

The first Lord Fairhaven purchased the Abbey in 1926. Against a background of humps and depressions formed by the old Priory, its moats and fish ponds, he created magnificent formal and romantic gardens. Avenues of rare coloured trees, poplars and chestnuts are separated by sweeping lawns and interspersed with classical statues, busts, urns and temples. In the spring there are wonderful displays of snowdrops, daffodils, narcissi, bluebells and hyacinths, in the summer the herbaceous borders are a delight and the year finishes with spectacular autumn colours.

Inside the house is the famous Fairhaven collection of furniture and paintings, the latter including works by Constable and Gainsborough and a collection of hundreds of paintings depicting Windsor Castle over a period of 350 years. They are all still displayed as Lord Fairhaven had first intended.

Both the Abbey and Lode Mill are owned by the National Trust and, whilst opening times vary, they are generally open between mid-March and mid-October, Wednesday to Sunday, 1.00pm to 5.00pm.

Acknowledgements

Grateful acknowledgement is made to the authors of publications listed under References and Further Reading together with the authors of numerous town, village, church and conservation guides. The author would like to further acknowledge all those who have given invaluable help and encouragement when researching this guide, including those in the Environment Agency, the Middle Level Commissioners, The Cam Conservancy, members of GOBA conservation bodies, tourist offices, libraries, museums, churches, marinas, and on footpaths, on boats and at locks.

Great Ouse Boating Association

More than 1,750 families enjoy the benefits of GOBA membership every year including….

★ Free overnight river moorings at more than 19 locations
  ★ A full colour magazine three times a year
  ★ Regular feedback with the River Authorities
  ★ A dedicated committee of seasoned boaters
  ★ Friendly help, advice and much more......

If you are not already a member why not join us now by completing and posting this application form or visit our website at www.goba.org for more information. We look forward to hearing from you.

✉ email membership@goba.org.uk
✉ GOBA, PO Box 244, Huntingdon, PE29 6FE
www.goba.org.uk

GOBA is registered under the Industrial and Provident Societies Acts in the United Kingdom and is run entirely by volunteers for the benefit of the Great Ouse boating community

---

DIRECT DEBIT

Please complete the whole form in BLOCK LETTERS using a ball point pen.

Instruction to your Bank or Building Society to pay by Direct Debit

Great Ouse Boating Association
PO BOX 244
HUNTINGDON
CAMBS
PE29 6 FE

Originators Identification Number

4	1	4	2	5	7

Reference Number (office use only)

G	O	B	A	-			

Name(s) of Account Holder(s)

Instruction to your Bank or Building Society

Please pay **Great Ouse Boating Association Ltd** Direct Debits from the account detailed in this Instruction subj ect to the safeguards assured by the Direct Debit Guarantee.

I understand that this instruction may remain with Great Ouse Boating Association Ltd and, if so, details will be passed electronically to my Bank/Building Society.

Bank / Building Society account number

Branch Sort Code

Name and full postal address of your Bank or Building Society

To the Manager

Bank/Building Society

Address

Postcode

Signature(s)

Date

Banks and Building Societies may not accept Direct Debit Instructions for some types of account

The Great Ouse Boating Association (GOBA) represents boaters on the river Great Ouse, Cam, Lark, Little Ouse, Wissey and associated East Anglian waterways of England. More than 40 years old, we have over 1,750 boating family members.

Our endeavour is to promote harmony between the various users of the river so that all may continue to share its peace and beauty. This may involve providing a representative on a local, regional or national committee such as the Parliamentary Waterways Group, pressing for retention of navigation, renting a mooring from an angling club or landowner, receiving and forwarding adequate notice of regattas, advising on the siting of riverside structures and vital facilities such as locks, water points and rubbish disposal.

GOBA provides to its boating members a means to put forward their needs to the statutory bodies controlling the waterways as well as use of GOBA 48 hour moorings free of charge, a three times yearly colour magazine giving up to date news of boating interest and regular bulletins posted at more than 70 GOBA notice boards and locks along the river.

GOBA is registered under the Industrial and Provident Societies Acts in the United Kingdom and is run entirely by a dedicated committee of seasoned boaters who volunteer their free time for the benefit of the Great Ouse boating community. We are also affiliated to the Royal Yachting Association (RYA).

Joining GOBA means a stronger association better able to speak on behalf of the boating community to maintain and even extend navigation on the Ouse.

This guarantee should be detached and retained by the Payer.

The Direct Debit Guarantee

DIRECT Debit

This Guarantee is offered by all Banks and Building Societies that take part in the Direct Debit scheme. The efficiency and security of the Scheme is monitored and protected by your own Bank or Building Society.

If the amounts to be paid or the payment dates change Great Ouse Boating Association Ltd will notify you 10 working days in advance of your account being debited or as otherwise agreed.

If an error is made by Great Ouse Boating Association Ltd or your Bank or Building Society, you are guaranteed a full and immediate refund from your branch of the amount paid.

You can cancel a Direct Debit at any time by writing to your Bank or Building Society. Please also send a copy of your letter to us.

April 2004 IMRAY

APPLICATION FOR MEMBERSHIP OF GOBA

Please complete the form in BLOCK LETTERS using the Direct Debit overleaf which greatly reduces the administration required of our volunteer workforce. If you really are unable to use the Direct Debit, make cheques or postal orders payable to GOBA Ltd.

Applications received after September will include membership for the following year (the last three months of the year are included free of charge). The annual subscription of £15 is payable in January of each year. Membership stickers are sent out in March with the Spring GOBA News magazine.

Please allow up to 28 days to receive your membership pack but in the meantime you may use our moorings on trust as soon as you have posted this application and provided you retain the other half as proof of posting and are prepared to show it if requested by a GOBA official.

Detach from your direct debit guarantee and send the completed form to: **GOBA New Membership, PO BOX 244, HUNTINGDON, CAMBS, PE29 6FE**

I / We wish to enrol as a member of the Great Ouse Boating Association in accordance with the Association's rules.

Mr (&) Mrs Ms Other:	Initial		Surname	
Address			Boat Name	
			Type	
Postcode			Length M	
EMAIL			Beam M	

Item	Qty	Price £	Total
First year membership*	1	17.00	17.00
GOBA Burgee		9.50	
Tie		9.50	
Enamel pin Badge		2.00	
		TOTAL £	

*Includes £2.00 joining fee.

Continued over the page